Georges de La Tour:
57 Colour Plates

By Maria Tsaneva

First Edition

*****

Georges de La Tour: 57 Colour Plates
*****

Copyright © 2015 by Maria Tsaneva

Foreword

Georges de La Tour (1593 – 1652) was a French Baroque painter, who spent most of his working life in the Duchy of Lorraine, which was temporarily absorbed into France between 1641 and 1648. He painted mostly religious chiaroscuro scenes lit by candlelight.

La Tour's s early work shows influences from Caravaggio, probably via his Dutch followers, and the genre scenes of cheats—as in The Fortune Teller —and fighting beggars clearly derive from the Dutch Caravaggisti, and probably also his fellow-Lorrainer, Jacques Bellange. These are believed to date from relatively early in his career.

La Tour is best known for the nocturnal light effects which he developed much further than his artistic predecessors had done, and transferred their use in the genre subjects in the paintings of the Dutch Caravaggisti to religious painting in his. Unlike Caravaggio his religious paintings lack dramatic effects. He painted these in a second phase of his style, perhaps beginning in the 1640s, using chiaroscuro, careful geometrical compositions, and very simplified painting of forms. His work moves during his career towards greater simplicity and stillness—taking from Caravaggio very different qualities than Jusepe de Ribera and his Tenebrist followers did. He often painted several variations on the same subjects, and his surviving output is relatively small.

He was born in the town of Vic-sur-Seille in the Diocese of Metz, which was part of the Holy Roman Empire, but had been ruled by France since 1552. Baptism documentation reveals that he was the son of Jean de La Tour, a baker, and Sybille de La Tour, née Molian. It has been suggested that Sybille came from a partly noble family. His parents had seven children in all, with Georges being the second-born.

La Tour's educational background remains somewhat unclear, but it is assumed that he travelled either to Italy or the Netherlands early in his career. He may possibly have trained under Jacques Bellange in Nancy, the capital of Lorraine, although their styles are very different. His paintings reflect the Baroque naturalism of Caravaggio, but this probably reached him through the Dutch Caravaggisti of the Utrecht School and other Northern (French and Dutch) contemporaries. In particular, La Tour is often compared to the Dutch painter Hendrick Terbrugghen.

In 1617 he married Diane Le Nerf, from a minor noble family, and in 1620 he established his studio in her quiet provincial home-town of Lunéville, part of the independent Duchy of Lorraine which was absorbed into France, during his lifetime, in 1641. He was given the title "Painter to the King" (of France) in 1638, and he also worked for the Dukes of Lorraine in 1623-4, but the local bourgeoisie provided his main market, and he achieved certain affluence. He was involved in a Franciscan-led religious revival in Lorraine, and over the course of his career he moved to painting almost entirely religious subjects, but in treatments with influence from genre painting.

Georges de la Tour and his family died in 1652 in an epidemic in Lunéville. After his death La Tour's work was forgotten until rediscovered by Hermann Voss, a German scholar, in 1915; some of La Tour's work had in fact been confused with Vermeer, when the Dutch artist underwent his own rediscovery in the nineteenth century. In the twentieth century a number of his works were identified once more, and forgers tried to help meet the new demand; many aspects of his work remain controversial among art historians.

Paintings

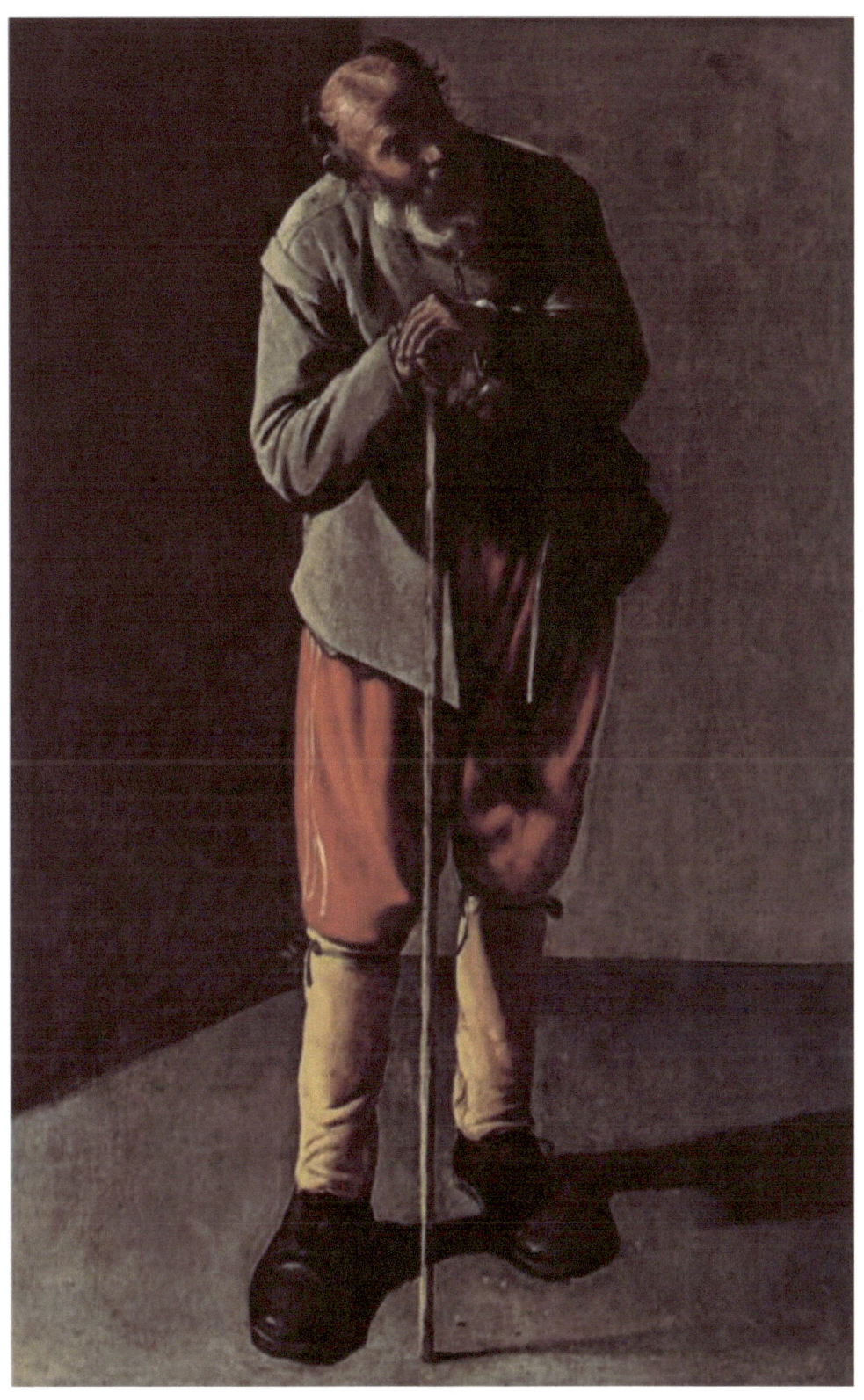

Old Man, c.1618-1619, oil on canvas

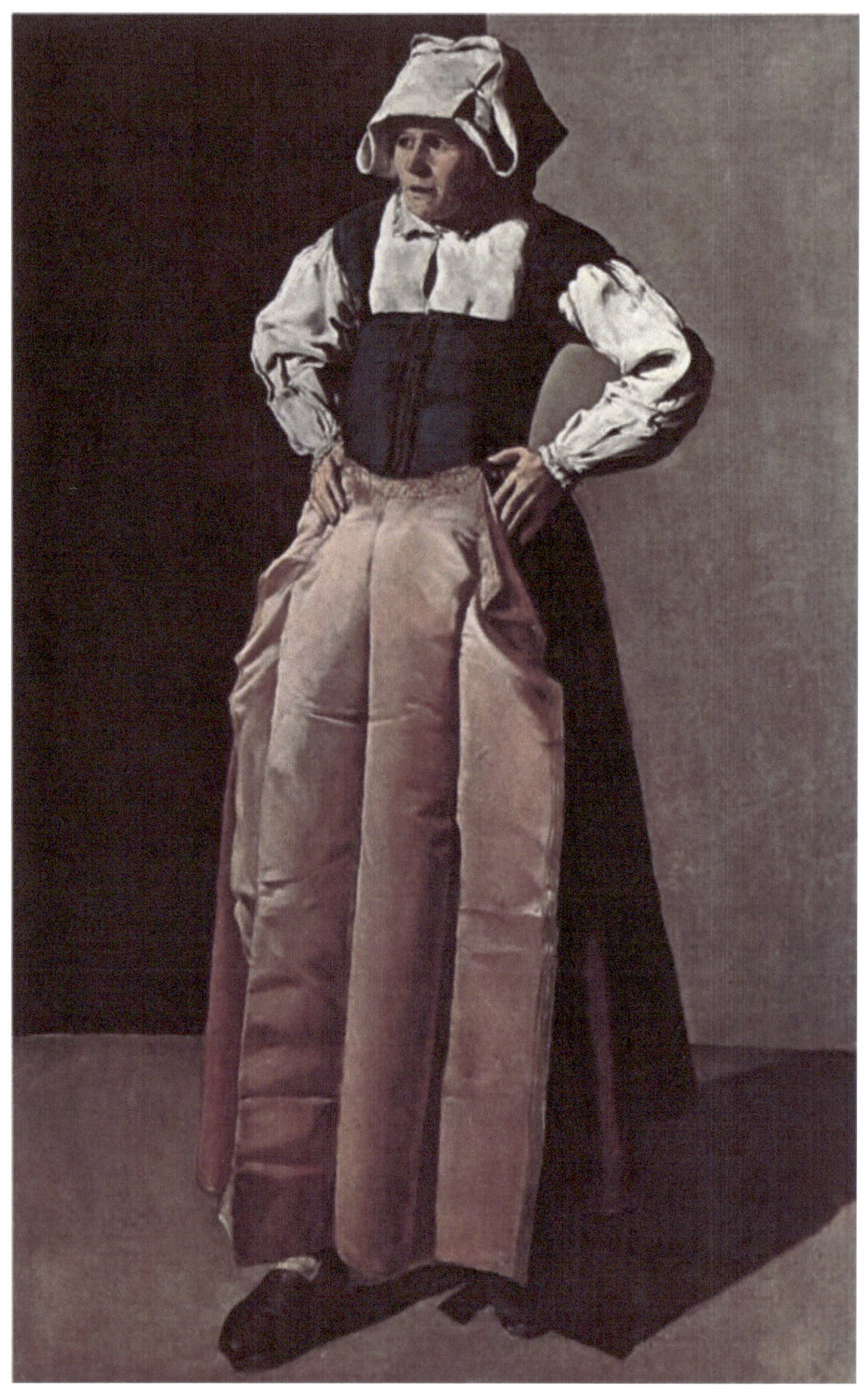

Old Woman, c.1618-1619, oil on canvas

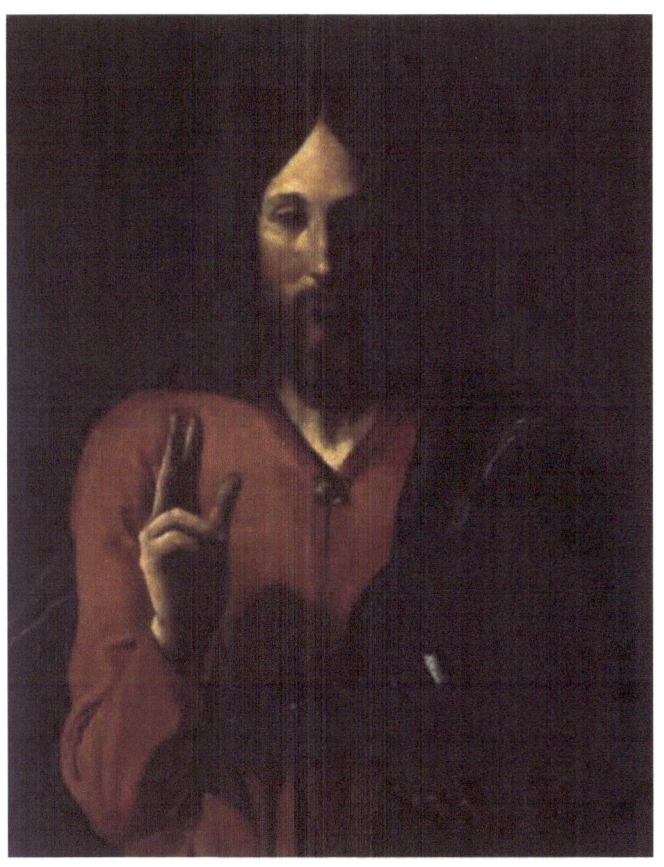

Christ Bénissant, 1615-1620, oil on canvas

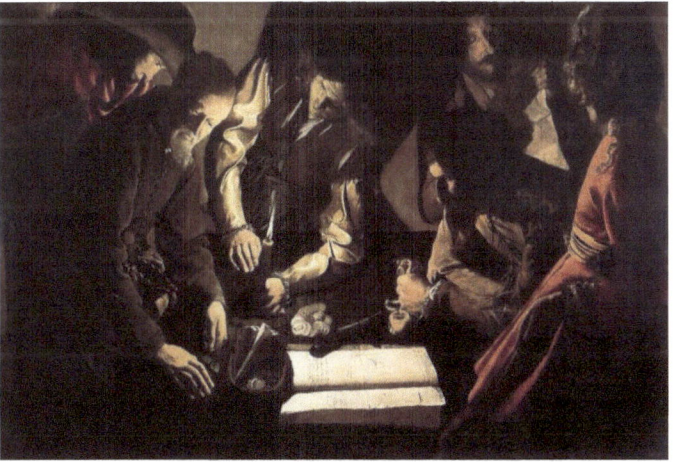

Payment of Taxes, c.1620, oil on canvas

An important early picture of La Tour is the surviving Payment of Dues, only identified in 1972, even though it has been in the museum at Lvov since at least the early nineteenth century. (Formerly the painting was attributed to Honthorst.) The picture was cleaned soon after its debut in Paris at the time of the La Tour exhibition in 1972, and a date was revealed. This date, thought to be 1634, has caused a great deal of controversy. If 1634 is correct, a drastic reassessment of La Tour's stylistic development must be made. The early pictures of saints remain from the 1620s, and then in the early 1630s La Tour moves towards his second phase, basically a Le Clerc-influenced period. The swaying figures and flickering lighting of the Payment of Dues are especially reminiscent of Le Clerc's Concert at Schleissheim. There is a certain ambiguity - often present in La Tour - in the subject, which appears to have been little studied. At first sight it is a simple peasant scene of the rich extracting money, ruthlessly, from the poor, but it could be a depiction of the 'Calling of Matthew' (the tax collector).

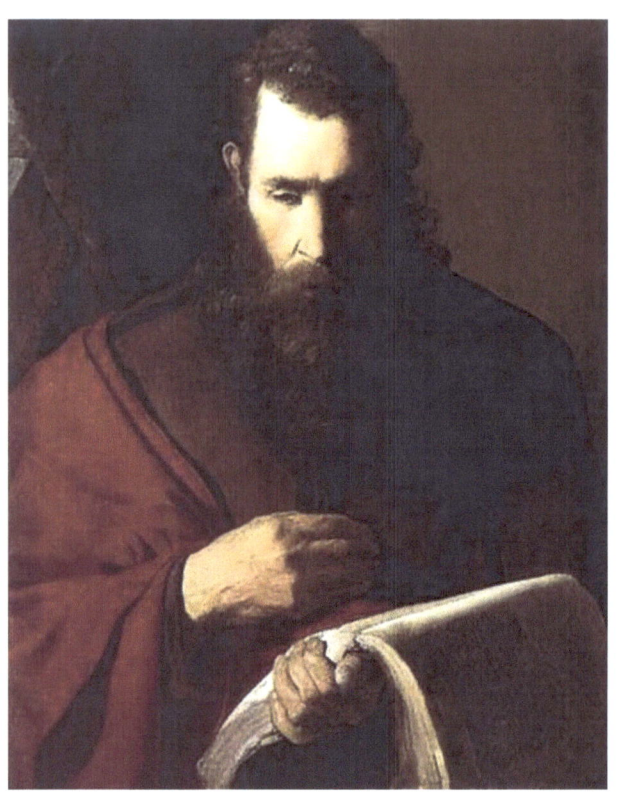

St. Andrew, 1615-1620, oil on canvas

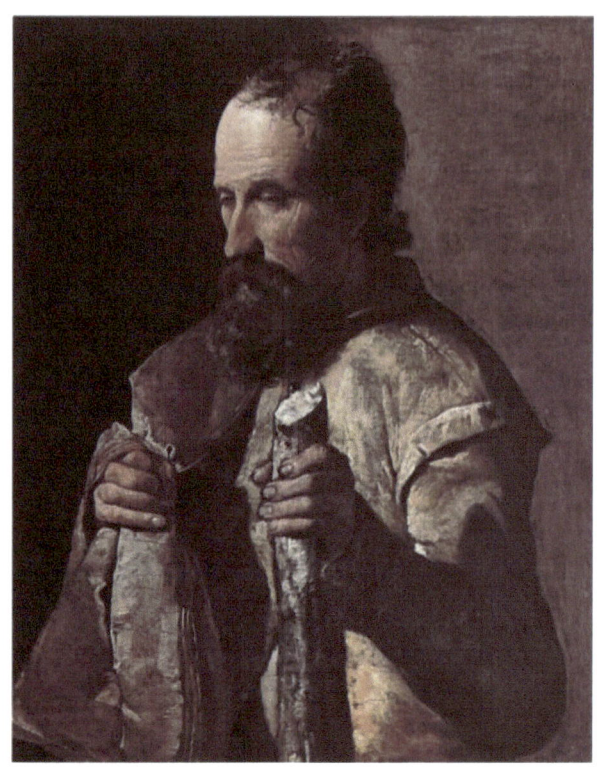

St. James the Minor, c.1615-c.1620, oil on canvas

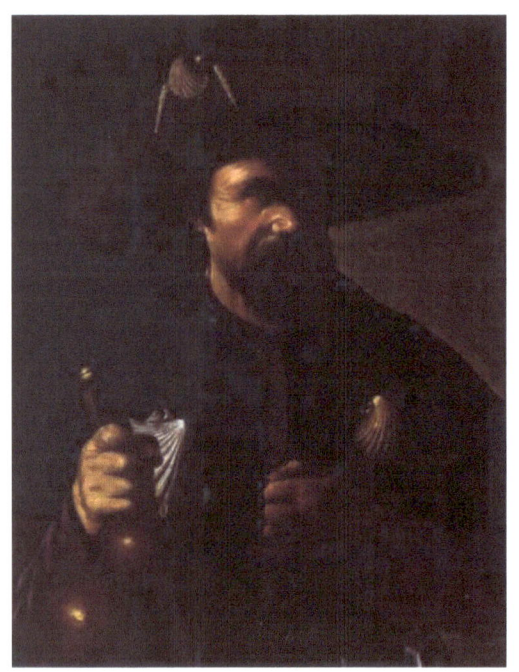

St. James the Greater, 1615-1620, oil on canvas

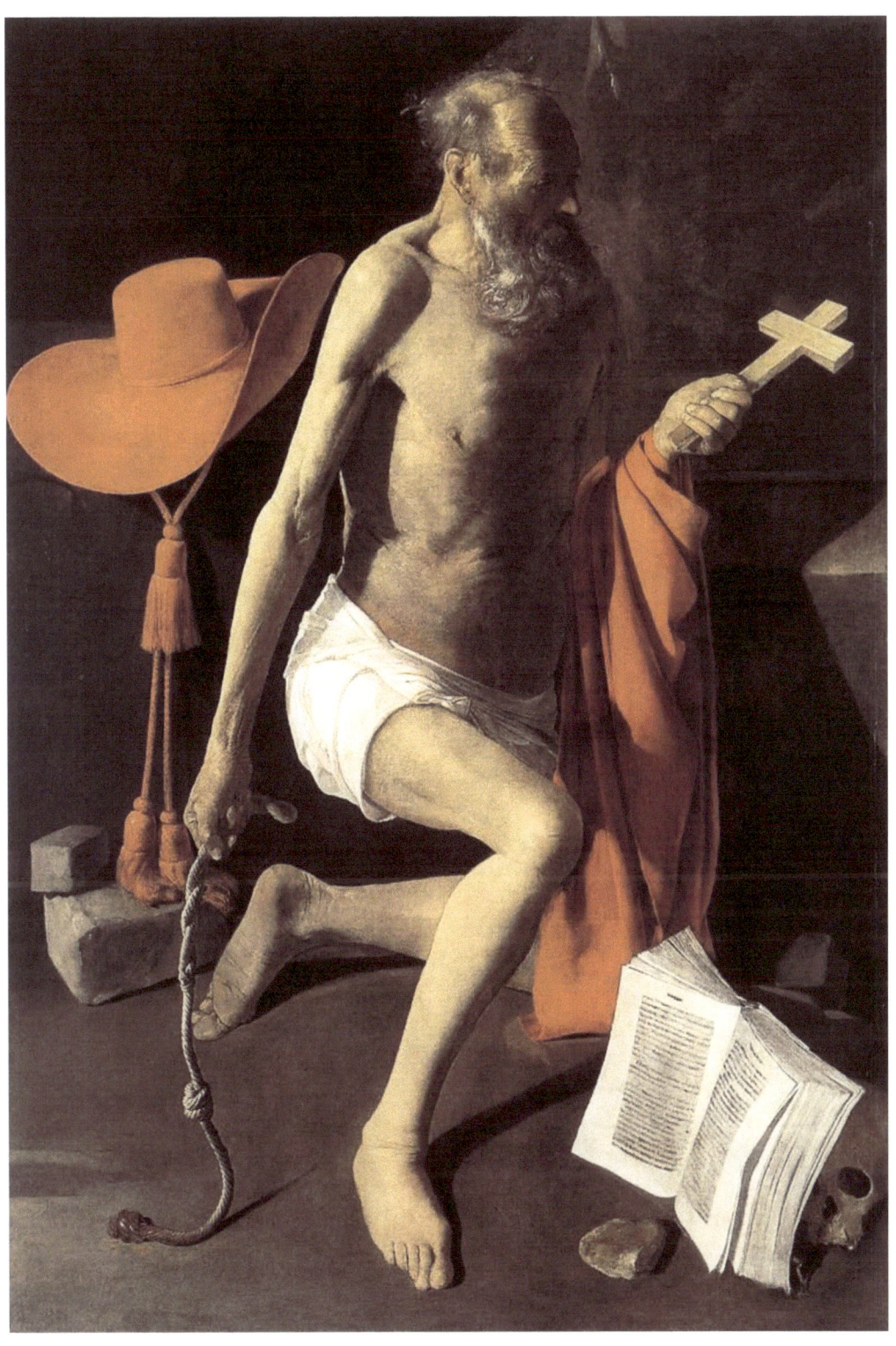

St. Jerome, c.1620, oil on canvas

A series of paintings by La Tour in the 1620s, including the St Jerome, shows that he came into contact with the style of Caravaggio. It is assumed that he went to Italy and picked up the tradition as it was continued in Rome by Manfredi and Valentin, but the particular form of naturalism in the St Jerome also suggests an acquaintance with Caravaggio's Dutch followers, especially with Terbrugghen's works.

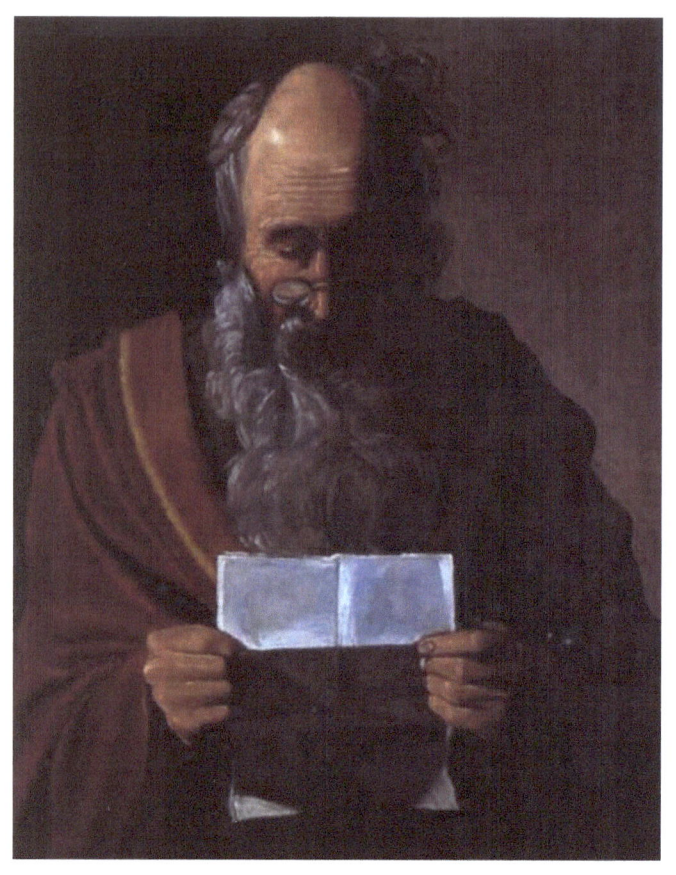

St. Paul, 1615-1620, oil on canvas

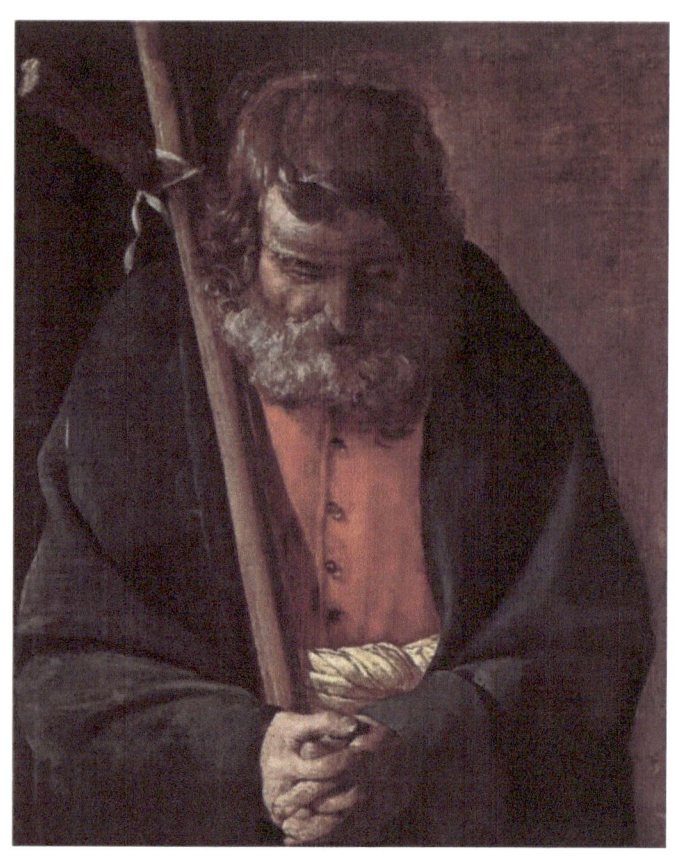

St. Philippe, c.1615-c.1620, oil on canvas

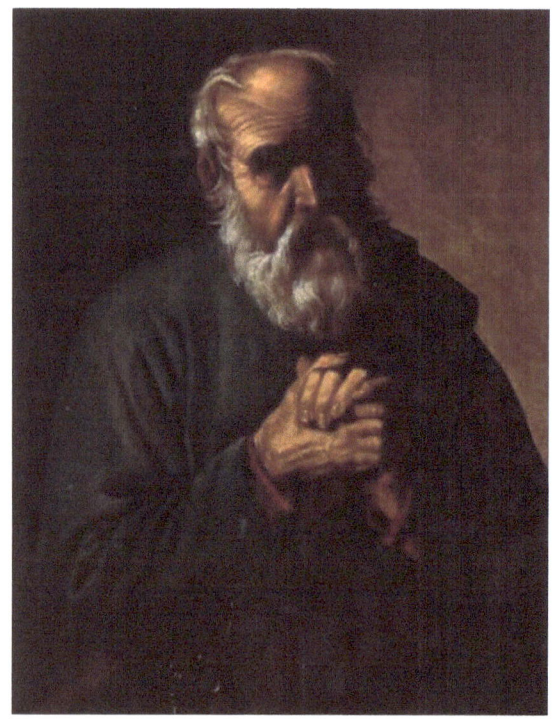

St. Peter, 1615-1620, oil on canvas

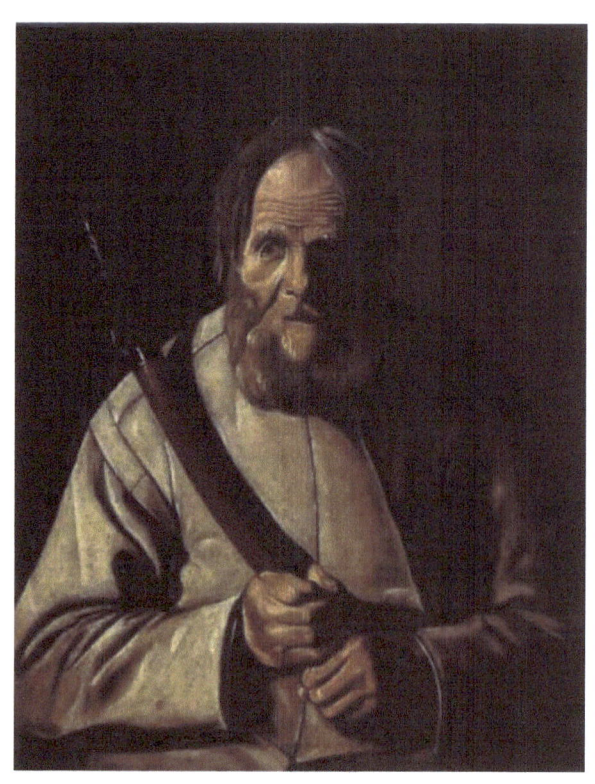

St. Simon, 1615-1620, oil on canvas

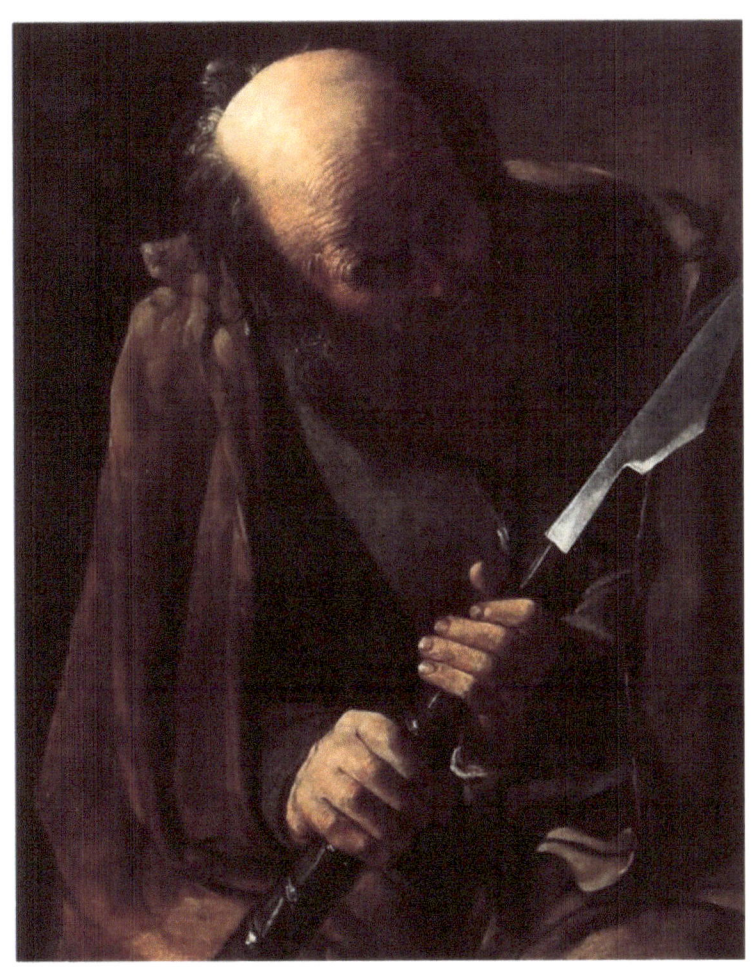

St. Thomas, c.1615–c.1620, oil on canvas

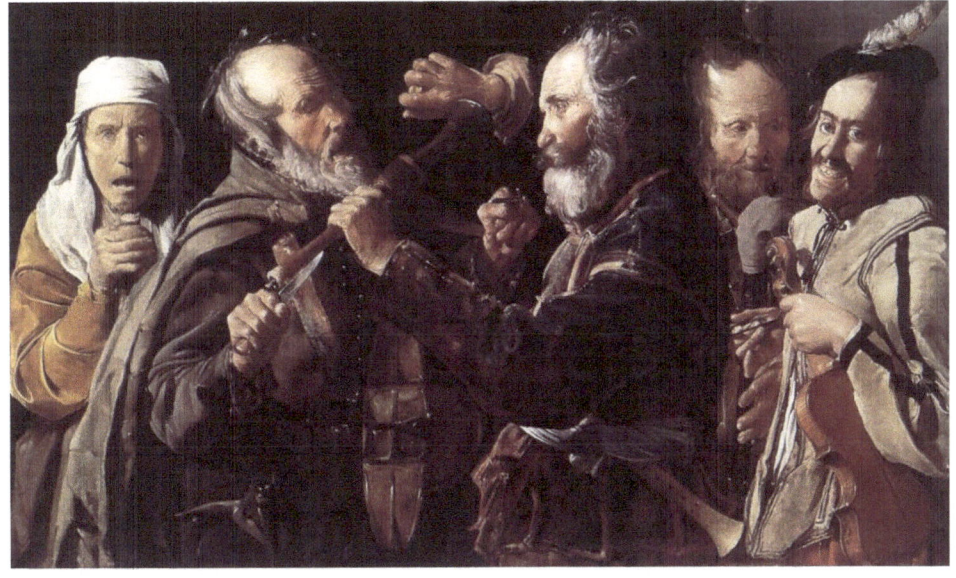

The Beggars' Brawl, 1620, oil on canvas

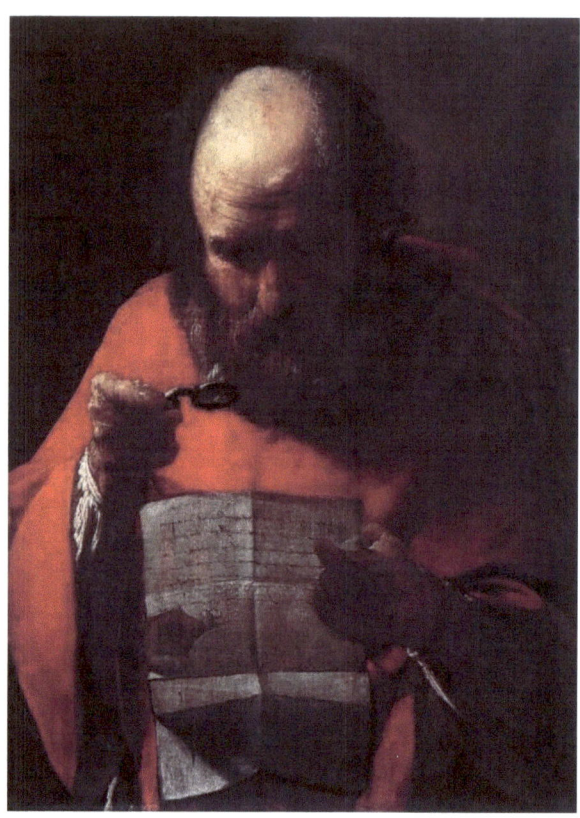

St. Jerome Reading, 1621-1623, oil on canvas

Charles II seems to have acquired this painting in 1662. At that time it was listed as 'St. Jerome wth [sic] spectacles of the manner of Albrecht Dьrer'; it was not until 1939 that it was recognised by Kenneth Clark as 'a very bad de la Tour'. Saint Jerome reading is now regularly discussed in the literature on the artist, whose popularity has risen dramatically in recent years. Having been born in Lorraine where he passed most of his life, de la Tour's style reveals a commingling of Italian and Northern Caravaggesque influences which suggest, but do not necessarily prove, visits to Rome and the Netherlands. However, his style remains determinedly individual and was equally the product of local influences. He was a man of independent means and was appointed Peintre Ordinaire du Roi in Paris in 1639.
There is a limited number of signed or dated works in the artist's small oeuvre and only approximate indications (some controversial) for the development of his style.
Saint Jerome reading may be compared with the series of Apostles at Albi (Musῐe Toulouse-Lautrec), usually regarded as early works although not all autograph. The figures of Saint James the Less, Saint Philip and Saint Paul are particularly relevant. Also significant is a variant Saint Jerome reading in Paris, a copy after a lost painting by de la Tour, which is a more sophisticated composition with the figure seen from above and numerous objects comprising a still-life in the foreground. A date of about 1621-23 has been suggested for all of these works, which herald the influence of Caravaggio.
Even allowing for the worn surface of the present painting, the chief characteristics of de la Tour's art can be discerned: the naturalistic rendering of hair and skin, the love of genre details such as the spectacles, the splash of saturated colour for the cardinal's robe and, above all, the mysterious light that illuminates the figure so powerfully. As a painter Georges de la Tour lifts the art of scientific observation onto a poetic level. It is not quite certain, for instance, to what degree the intense luminosity renders the paper transparent, but it helps to define the distance between the viewer and Saint Jerome in the picture space while providing a bright focal point on a vertical axis. The concentration that characterises Saint Jerome gradually envelops the viewer to the extent that the internal act of reading becomes synonymous with the external discipline of looking.

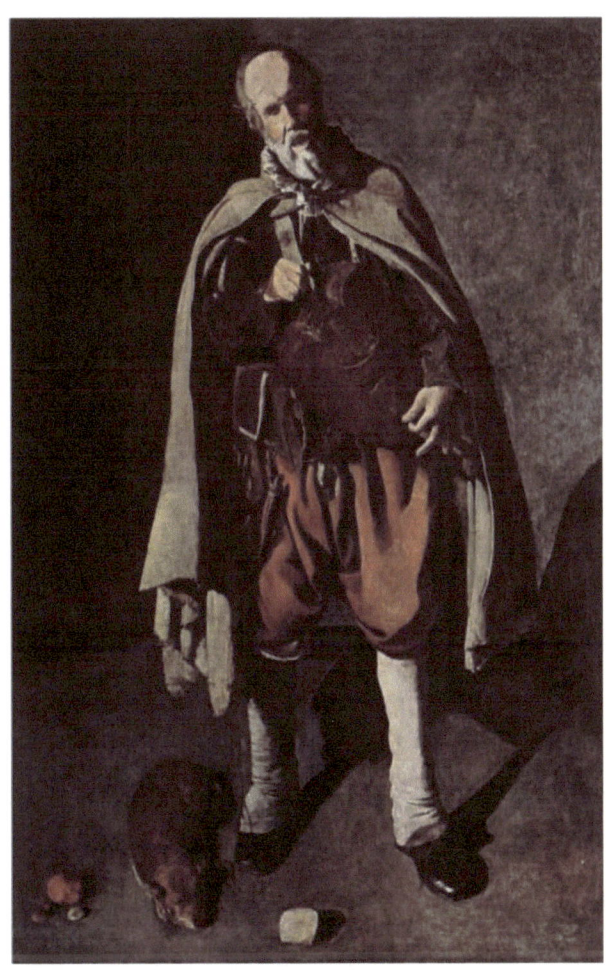

The Hurdy-Gurdy Player with a Dog, c.1622-c.1625, oil on canvas

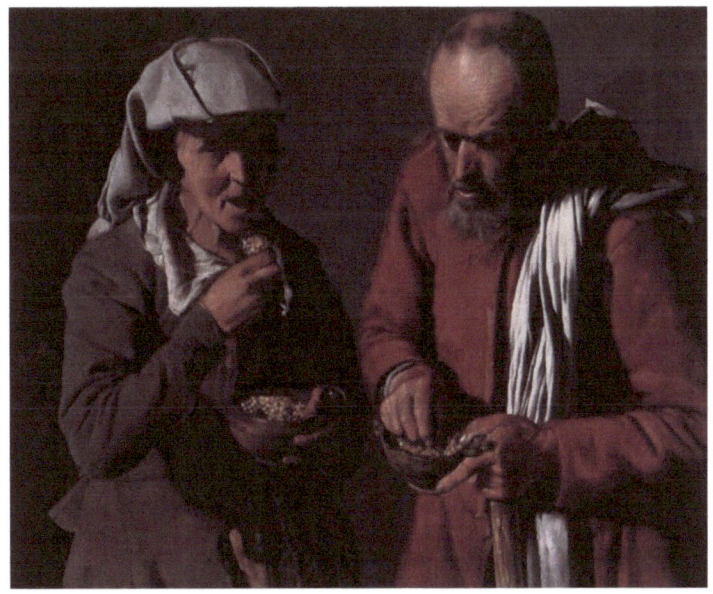

The Porridge Eaters, c.1622-c.1625, oil on canvas

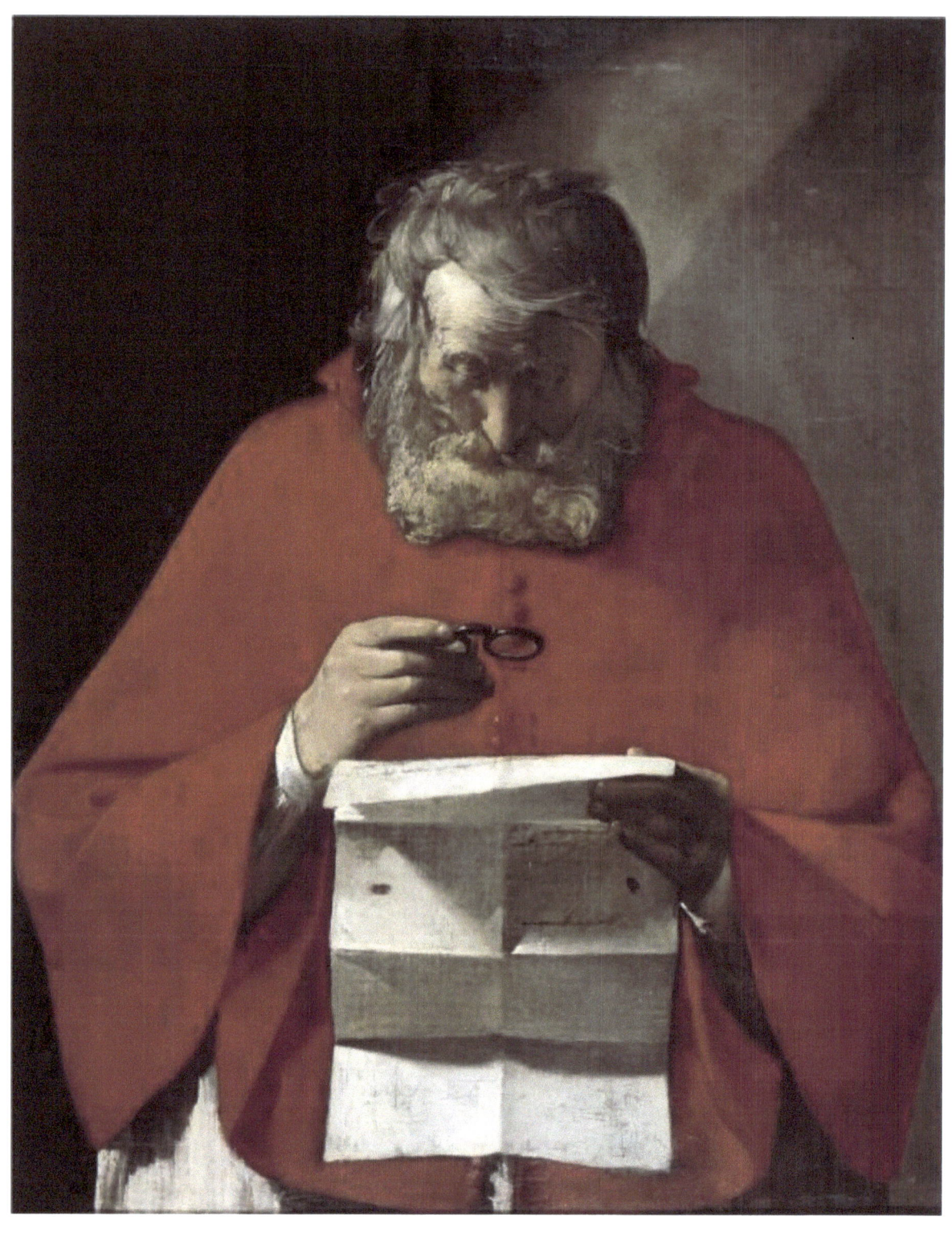

Saint Jerome reading a letter, 1627-1629, oil on canvas

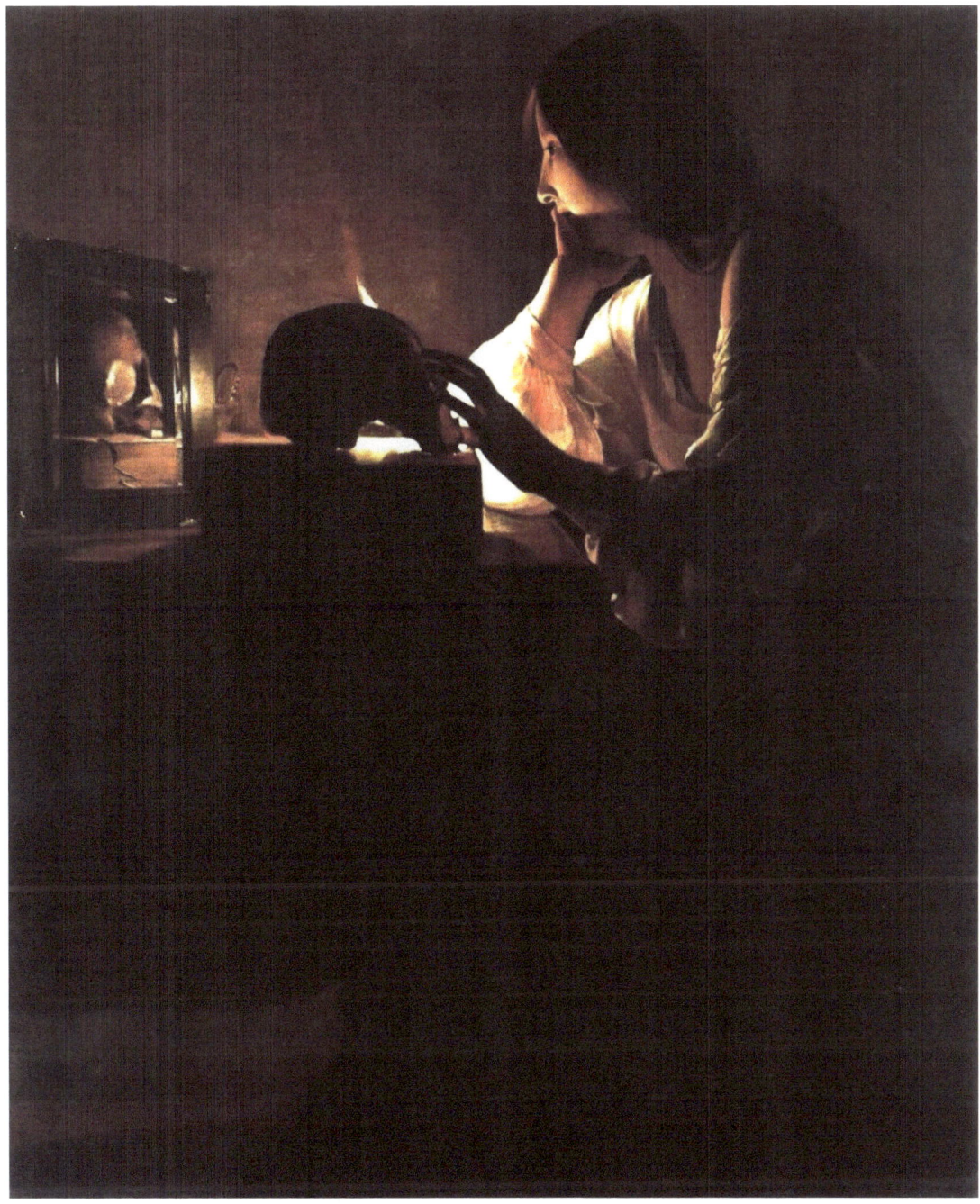

Repenting Magdalene, also called Magdalene before Mirror or Magadalene Fabius., c.1630, oil on canvas

The repentant (penitent) Magdalen was a theme of particular importance for Georges de La Tour. He is known to have painted four full-length versions of the subject which are now in the Metropolitan Museum of Art, New York; in the Musee du Louvre, Paris; in the Los Angeles County Museum of Art, Los Angeles; and in the National Gallery of Art, Washington. Moreover, there are several copies as well as a contemporary engraving.

All of La Tour's Magdalens run counter to the type favoured by most of his contemporaries, who preferred to portray a voluptuous and scantily clothed Magdalen in a cave or grotto, eyes heavenward, curly blond hair flowing over her shoulders. By contrast, La Tour's Magdalens appear in profile with dark, straight hair, seated at a table in an austere interior.

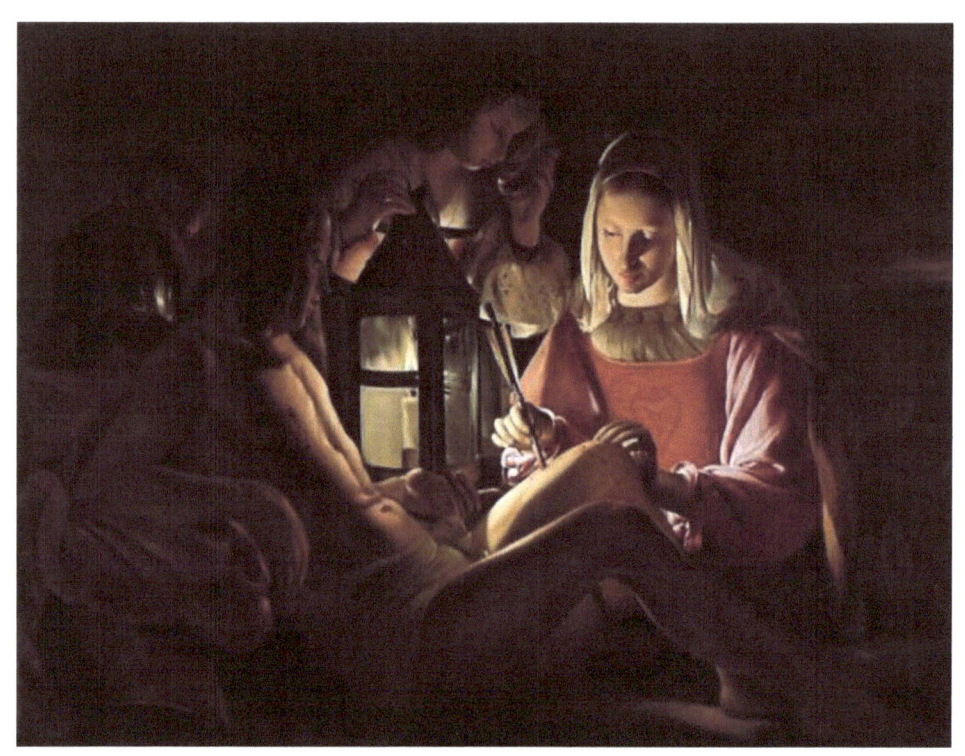

St. Sebastian with Lantern, c.1630, oil on canvas

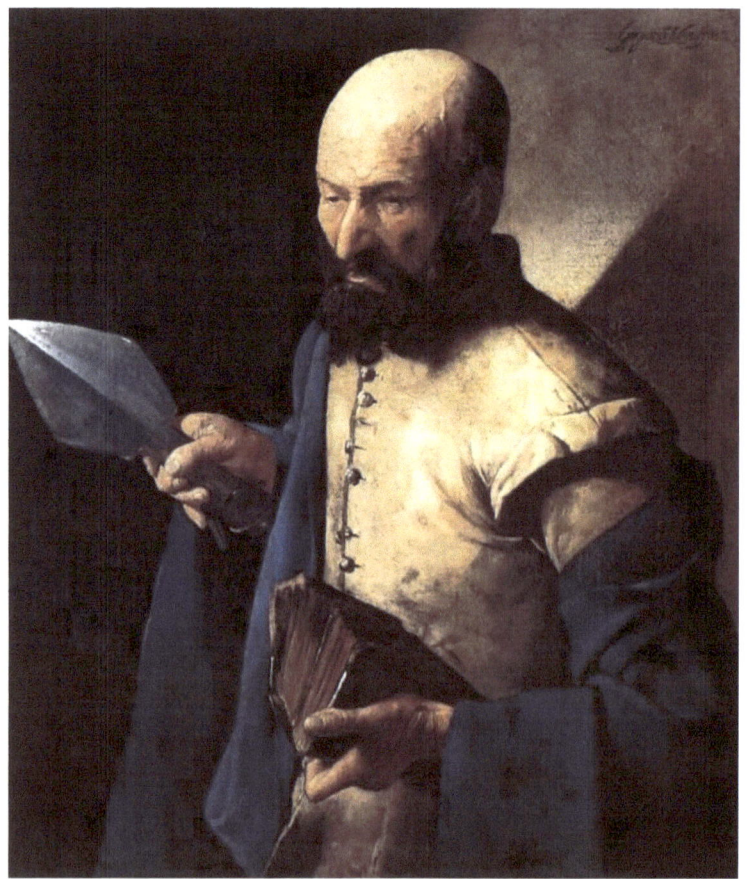

St. Thomas, also called Saint with a Pike, 1625-1630, oil on canvas

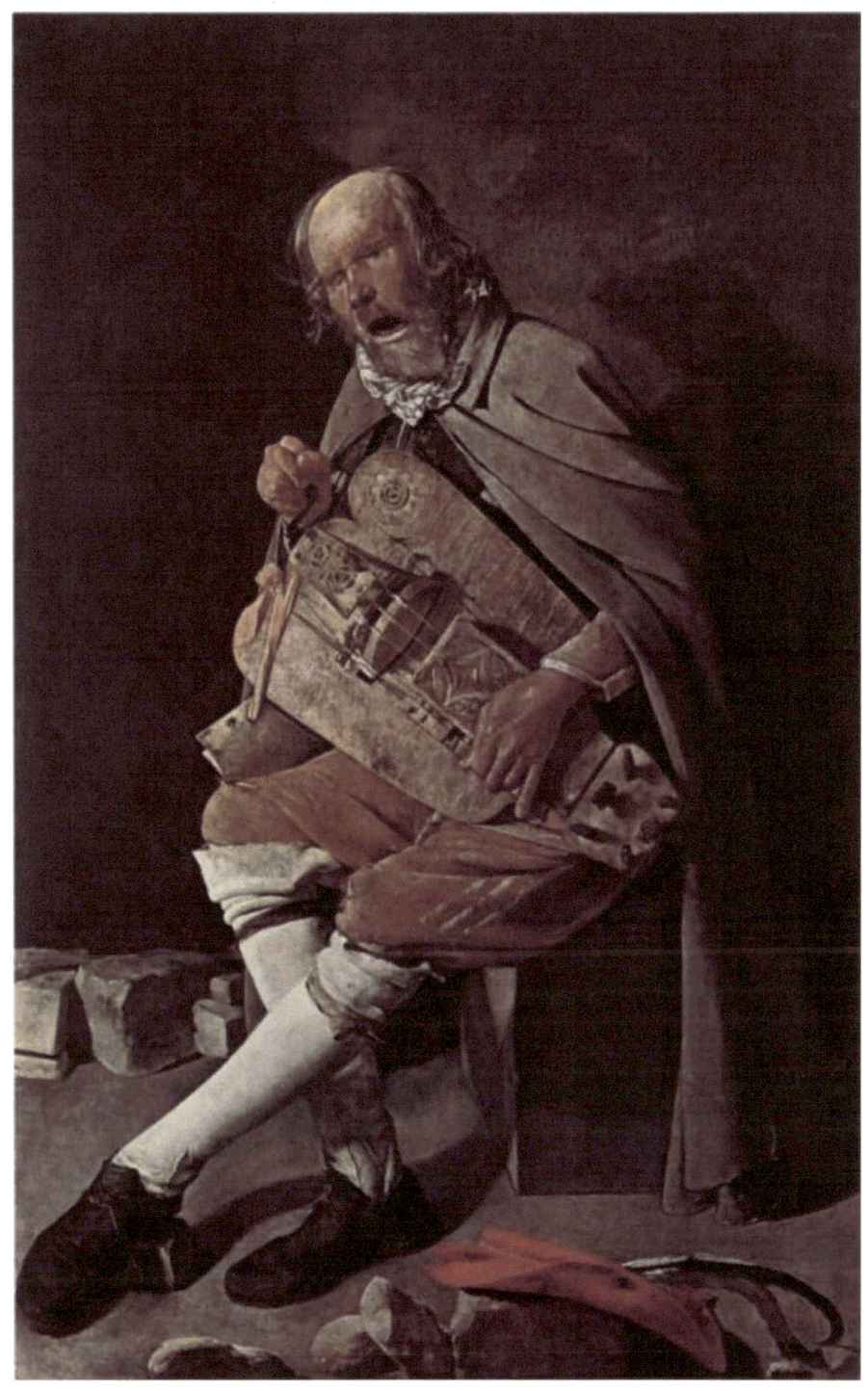

The Hurdy-Gurdy Player, also called Hurdy-Gurdy Player with Hat, c.1620-c.1630, oil on canvas

The representation of popular music, played mainly in the street and featuring instruments which were typical of this type of music, appeared in Rome in the 1620s emerging from Flemish and French painting. The most important examples of this genre include the Hurdy-gurdy Player by Georges de La Tour. The attribution to Georges de La Tour is dubious. However, this work has the same picturesque, rugged, descriptive quality as the St Jerome in Stockholm, and it is painted from a very similar model.

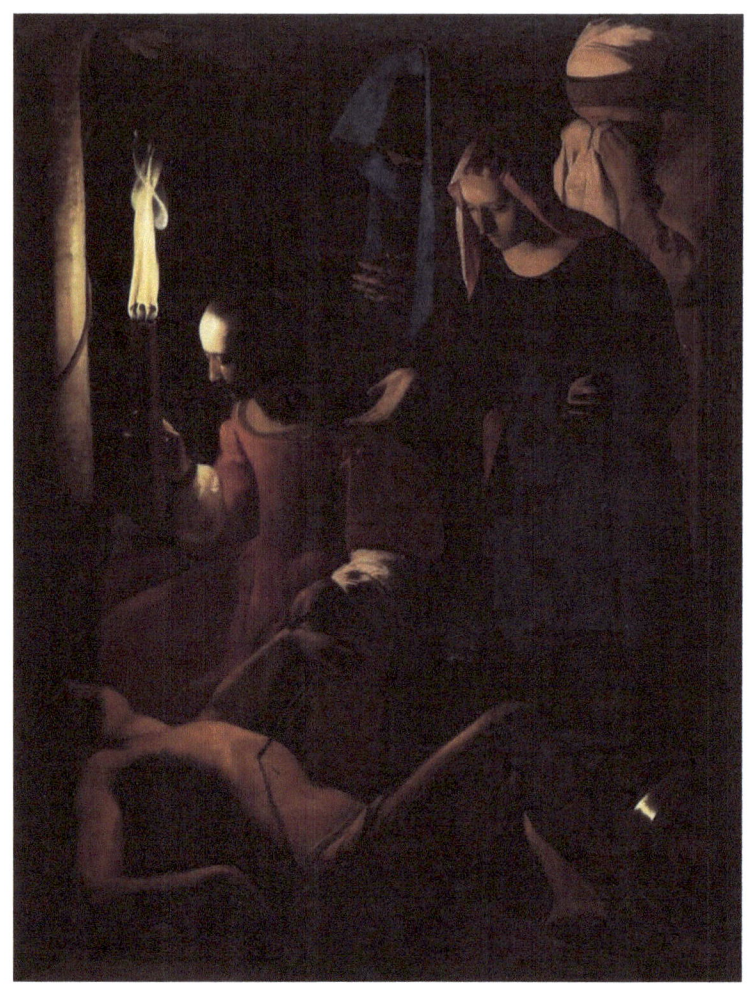

St Sebastien Attended by St Irene, 1634-43, Oil on canvas, 160 x 129 cm

There is a group of painting attributed to Georges de La Tour depicting St Sebastian and St Irene. Part of them is a horizontal composition where the model of one of the figures is a familiar La Tour type. Most of the versions are curiously incompetent, only three of them having pretensions to quality. The upright versions of the same subject (one in the Louvre and the other in Berlin) are more celebrated. The composition is monumental, as if the painting were depicting a sculptured tableau.

The Louvre composition is especially moving, with the mourning figure in a blue cowl (in the Berlin version the cowl is black) looking as if she were taken from a piece of Burgundian tomb sculpture. Recent observations on the possible dating of the costumes have left little doubt that the picture is rather later than the artist's lifetime. Ŭtienne de La Tour, the son of the artist was suggested (but not accepted) as the possible author. Ŭtienne de La Tour is actually documented as being required to continue his father's style should the latter die inopportunely, and it is likely that he continued long into the 1660s and even the 1670s, painting ever-weaker versions of his father's work which eventually became mockeries of his father's genius.

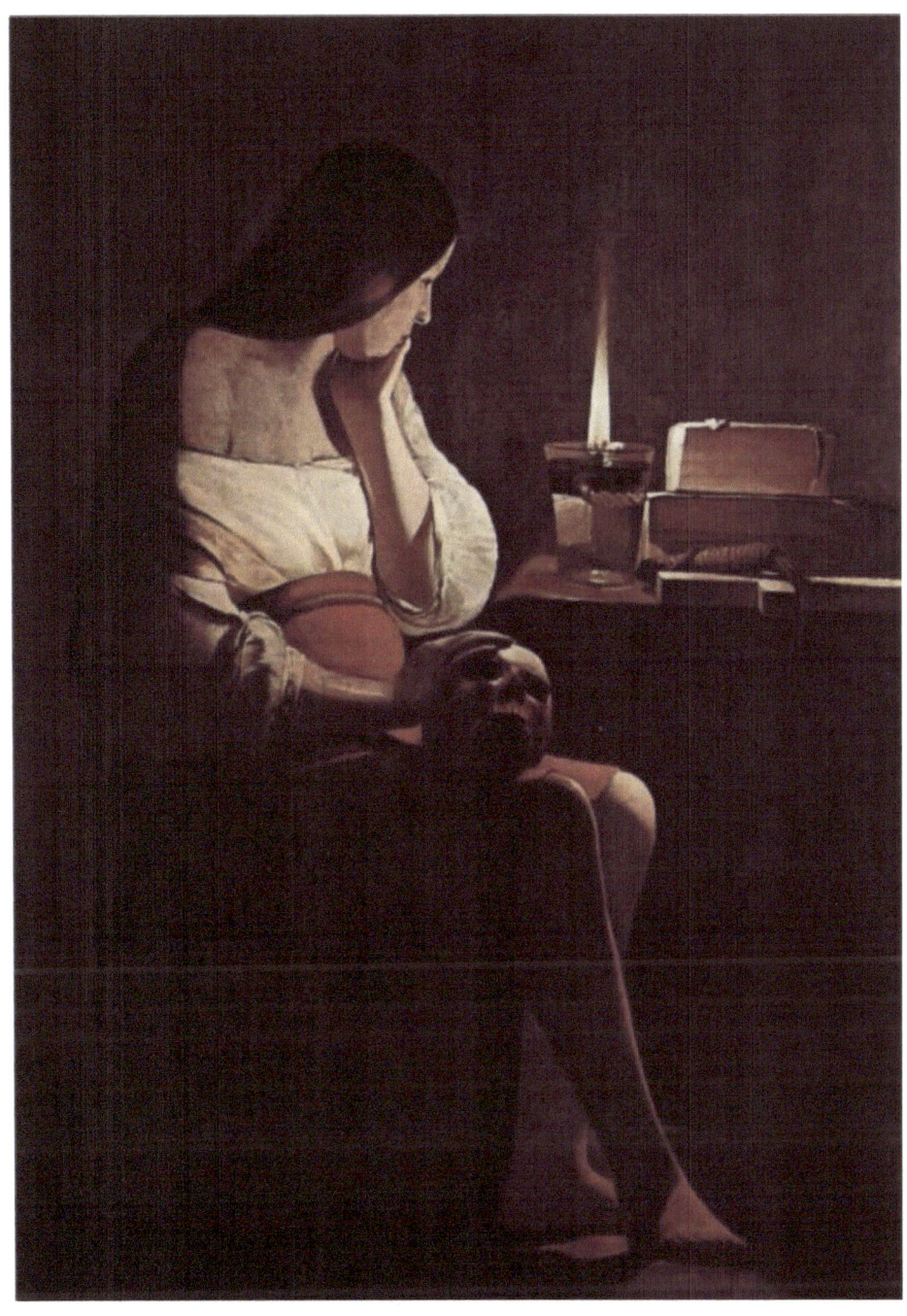

Mary Magdalene with a night light, 1630-1635, oil on canvas

Magdalen was the object of great devotion in France and La Tour painted several pictures representing her.

Georges de La Tour was successful during his lifetime, however he remains somewhat mysterious. A journey to Italy during his youth before he settled at Lunйville, may explain his Caravaggism. Without much imagination, he has very personal colour effects; a fine red often recurs in the nocturnal atmosphere of his pictures, in which the long candle, often seen in transparence, lights up thick, voluntarily geometrical volumes, in the melancholy resignes loneliness of his models.

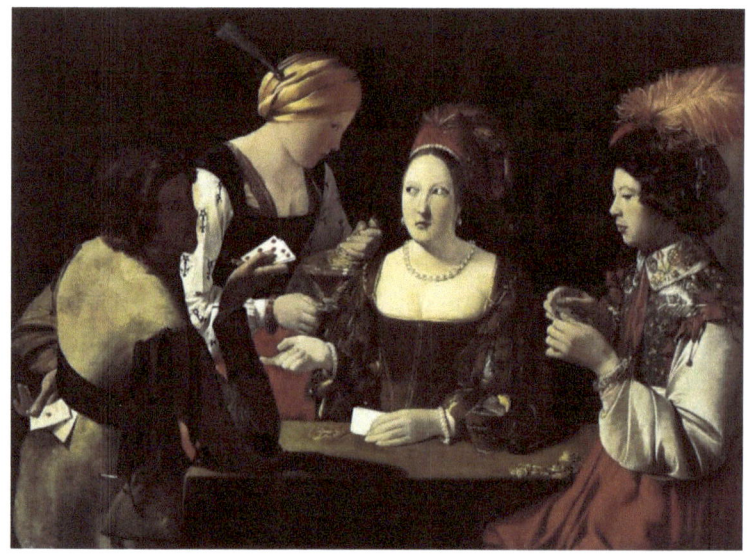

The Cheat with the Ace of Diamonds, 1635, oil on canvas

Georges de La Tour perfected the technique to carry banal or clownish scenes to an astonishingly delectable and sometime sublime state. The posturings of the dupes and scoundrels in the Cheater with the Ace of Diamonds confirm the artist's attachment to mocking scenes rendered in a dense, dazzling manner. The malicious cheating that occurs in this painting is admirably enhanced by costumes, movements, glances, poses, and even headwear. This is a version of Caravaggesque gambling scenes - morally more sinister but more glamorous and droll to look at.

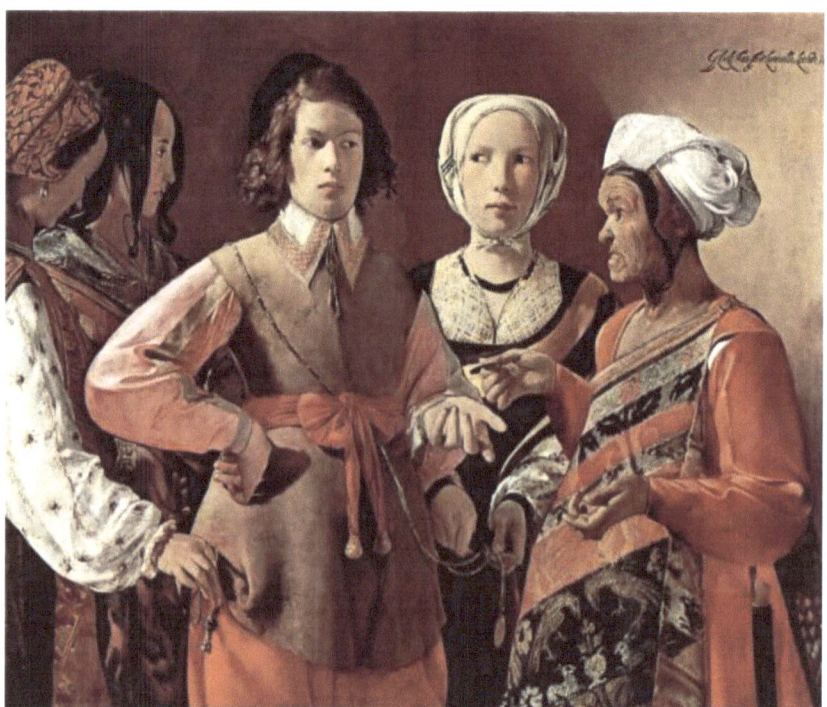

The Fortune-Teller, c.1632-c.1635, oil on canvas

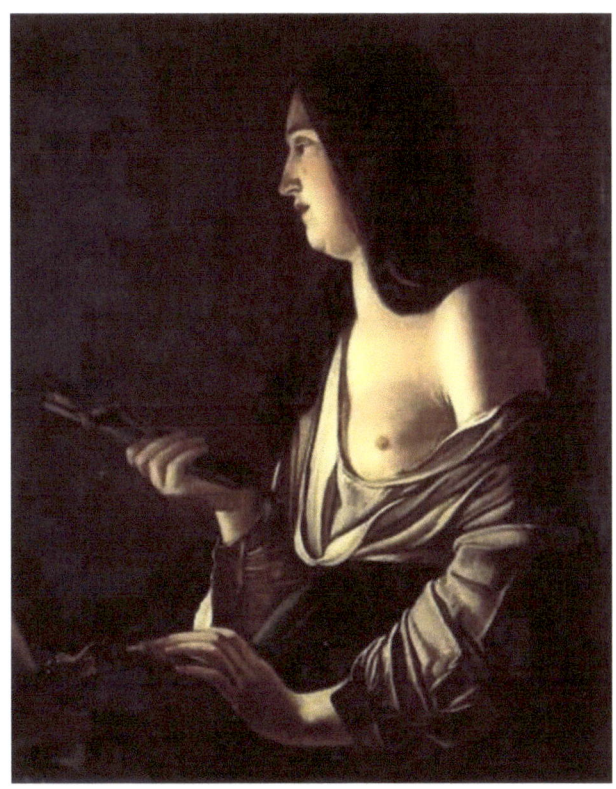

Repenting Magdalene, also called Magdalene in a Flickering Light, 1635-1637, oil on canvas

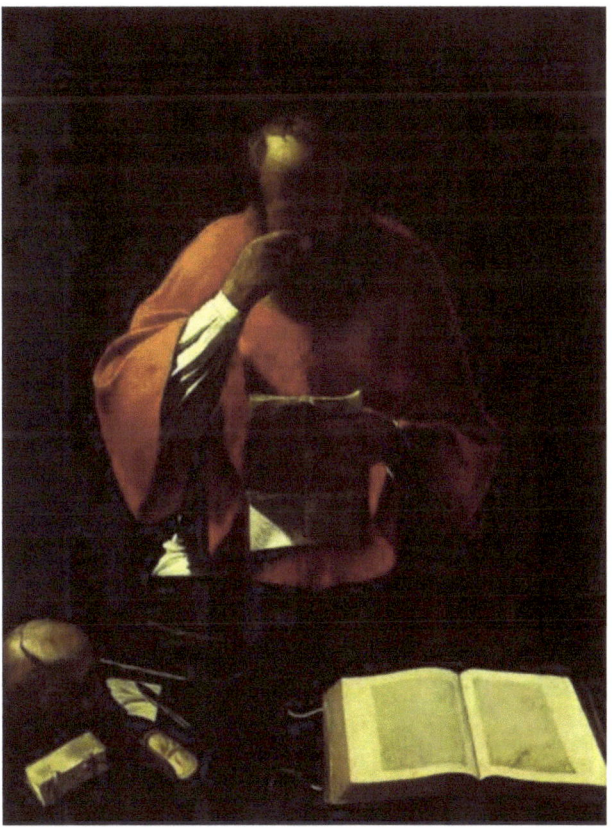

St.Jerome reading, c.1635-1638, oil on canvas

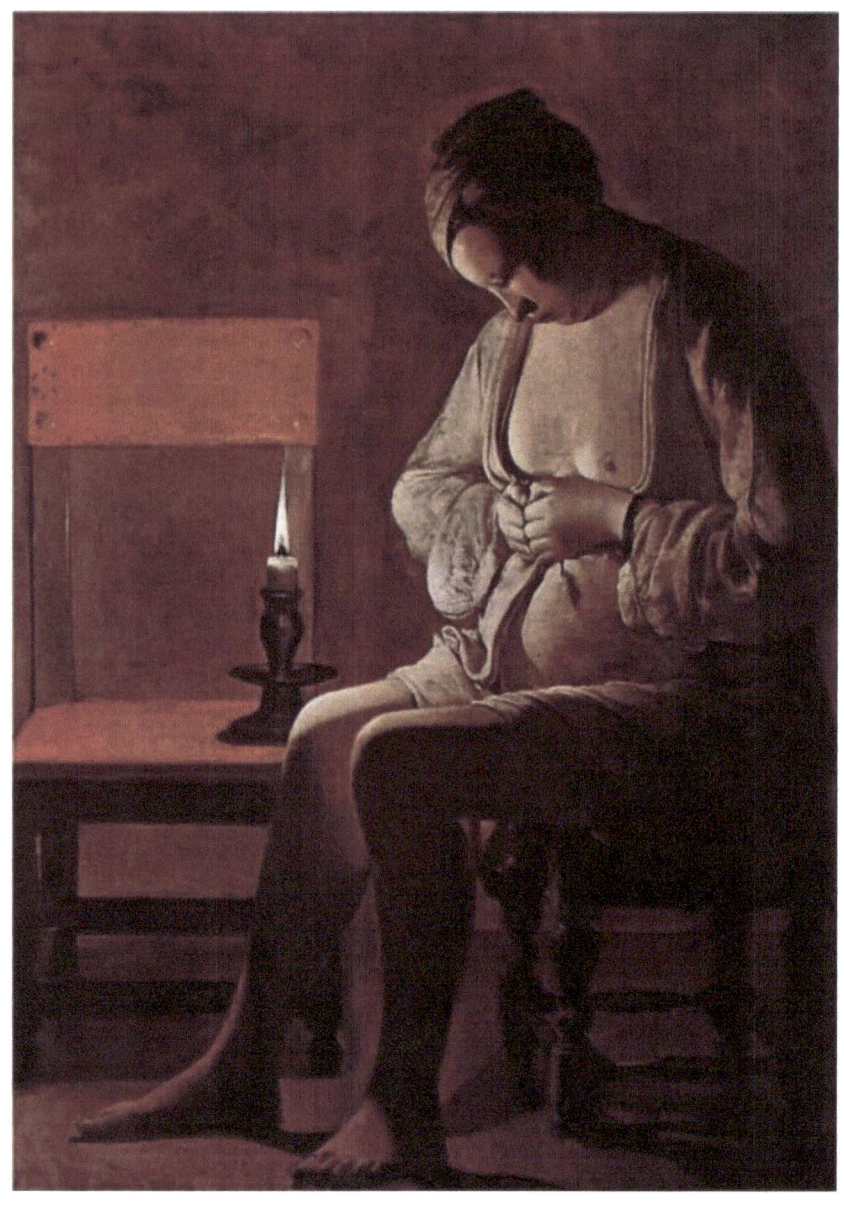

Woman Catching a Flea, c.1638, oil on canvas

La Tour, as with Rembrandt and Velazquez, made the most creative use of the lessons of Caravaggism. This painting combines chiaroscuro and candlelight with an uncompromising realism, and achieves a surprising intimacy of feeling.

This painting is enigmatic in both composition and subject-matter. It strikes an uneasy note because of its stark simplicity, which has usually been interpreted as a genre scene of low life - a woman crushing a flea between her fingernails - but no authentic La Tour depicts such an obviously banal theme without a deeper meaning. The only symbol in the picture is the solitary candle burning on the chair, and it is surely not too speculative to suggest that the picture might reprsent the pregnant Virgin, isolated by Joseph when he discovers that she is with child, the candle thus symbolizing the forthcoming Christ as the Light of the World.

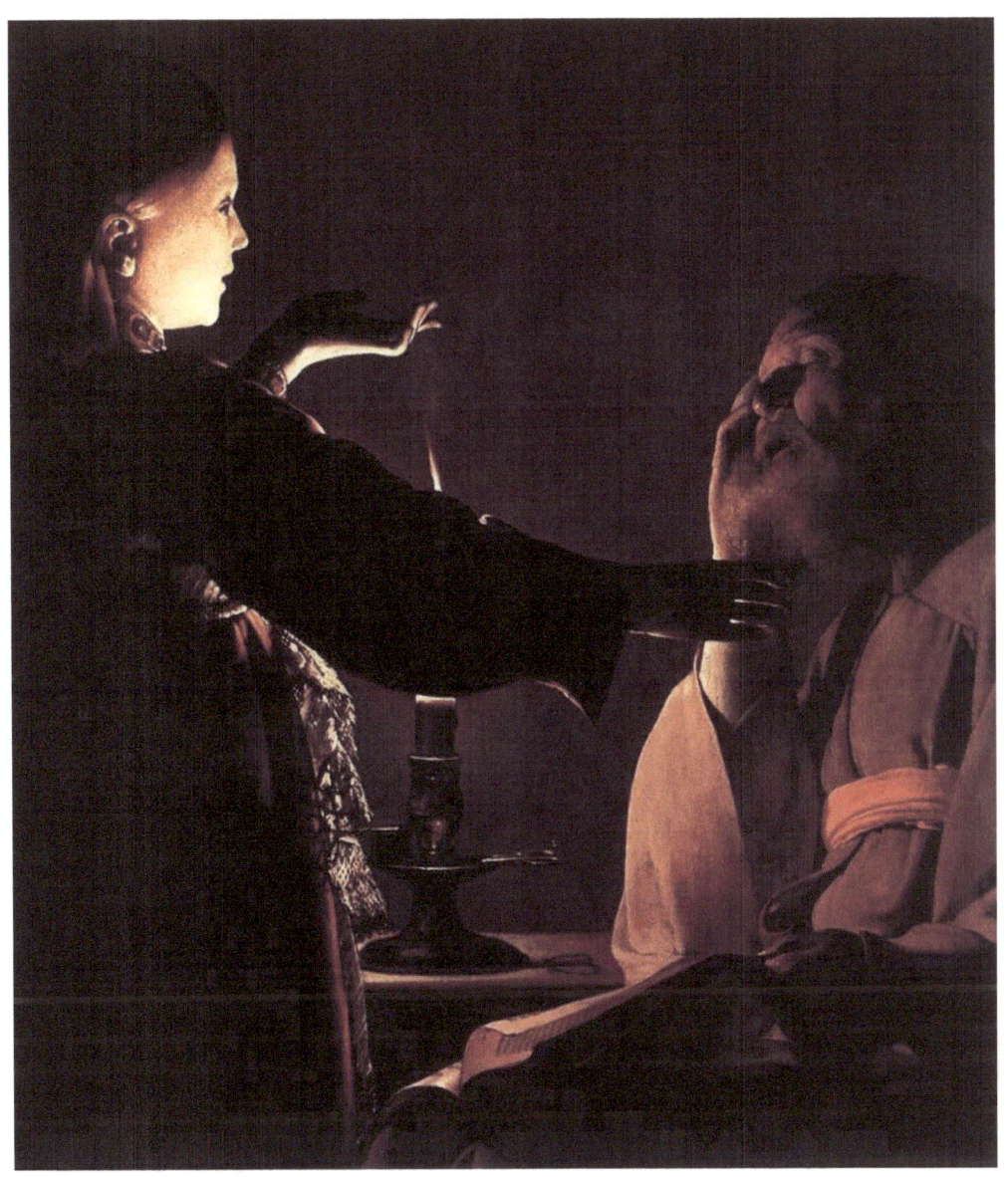

Appearance of Angel to St. Joseph, also called The Dream of St Joseph, c.1640, oil on canvas

La Tour's mature pictures form a close-knit group which must date from the years immediately before and after 1640. None of them is documented, although some of them are signed. The most typical and one of the best preserved of them is the so-called Dream of Joseph at Nantes, which in many respects forms a microcosm of La Tour's art and the problems which surround it, in terms of both history and the interpretation of the subject.

As recently as 1913 it was attributed to Rembrandt, although the picture was clearly signed La Tour in the top right-hand corner. It is interesting that an illustrious name should have been sought for so magical a picture, and the subject, even now, is as elusive as was the former difficulty of attribution. A youth in biblical costume is making a beckoning or announcing gesture before an old man who has fallen asleep reading a book. The traditional interpretation is that it is a Dream of Joseph, even though Joseph is normally shown as a carpenter (as he is in La Tour's Louvre picture). The youth is hardly the angel Gabriel either, coming to warn Joseph to flee to Egypt in order to escape the impending massacre of all children in Bethlehem by Herod's soldiers.

A possible explanation for this enigmatic picture is that it depicts the moment when the young Samuel, having been, he thinks, summoned by the elderly priest Eli, finds him asleep. This surprises Samuel, who at that instant realizes that it is God's voice calling him. If this interpretation of the subject is correct, La Tour has with characteristic subtlety and understatement shown the exact moment when the youth Samuel arrives before the sleeping old man, with a 'here I am' gesture. Samuel's pose is unforgettable. All attempts at the naturalism with which La Tour is so wrongly credited have been abandoned, leaving a Mannerist twisting of the fingers and the caprice of shielding most of the candle flame. Above all, there is an exquisite stillness, which pervades not only this picture but also the other all-too-few masterpieces from this period.

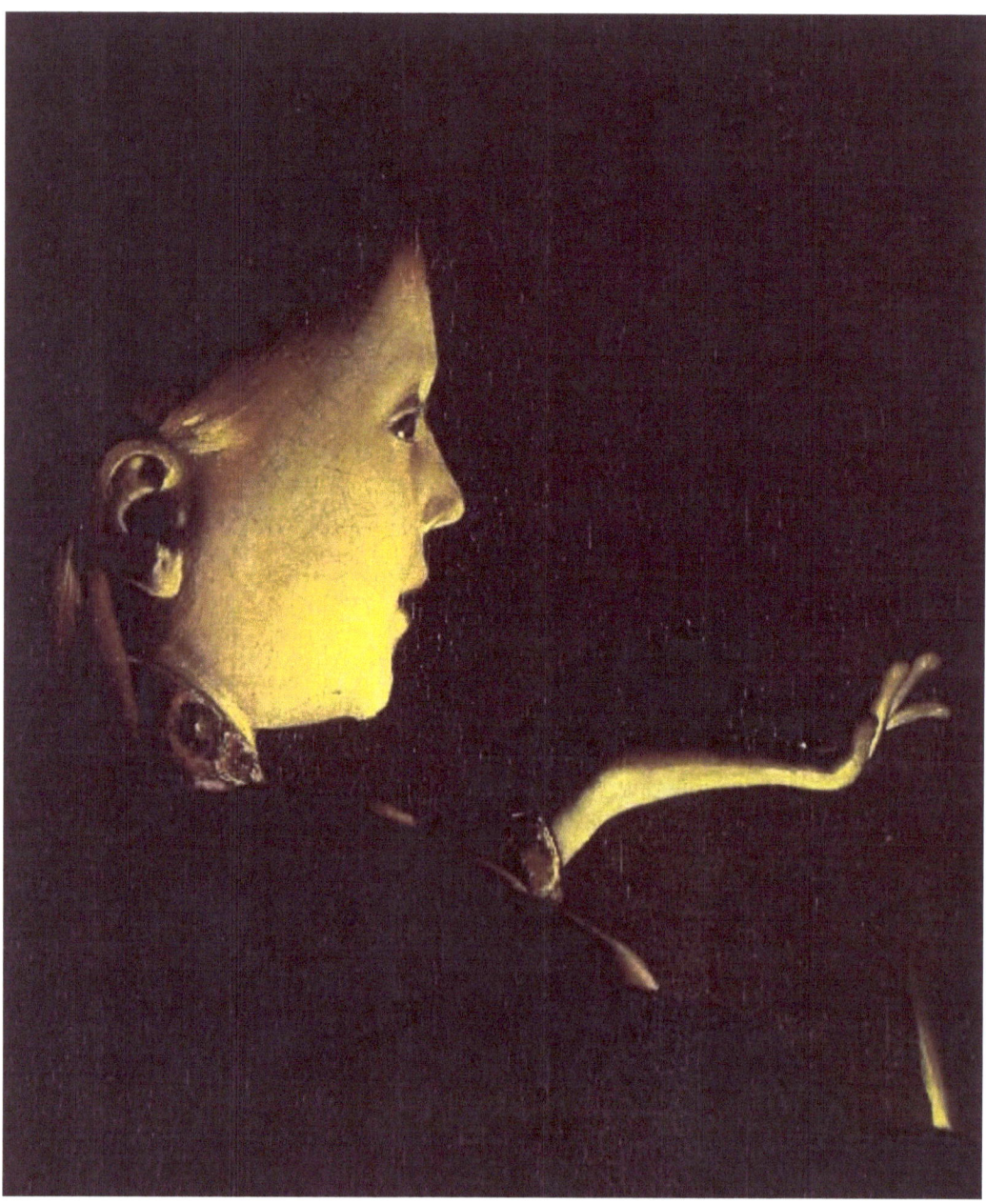

The Dream of St Joseph (detail), c. 1640

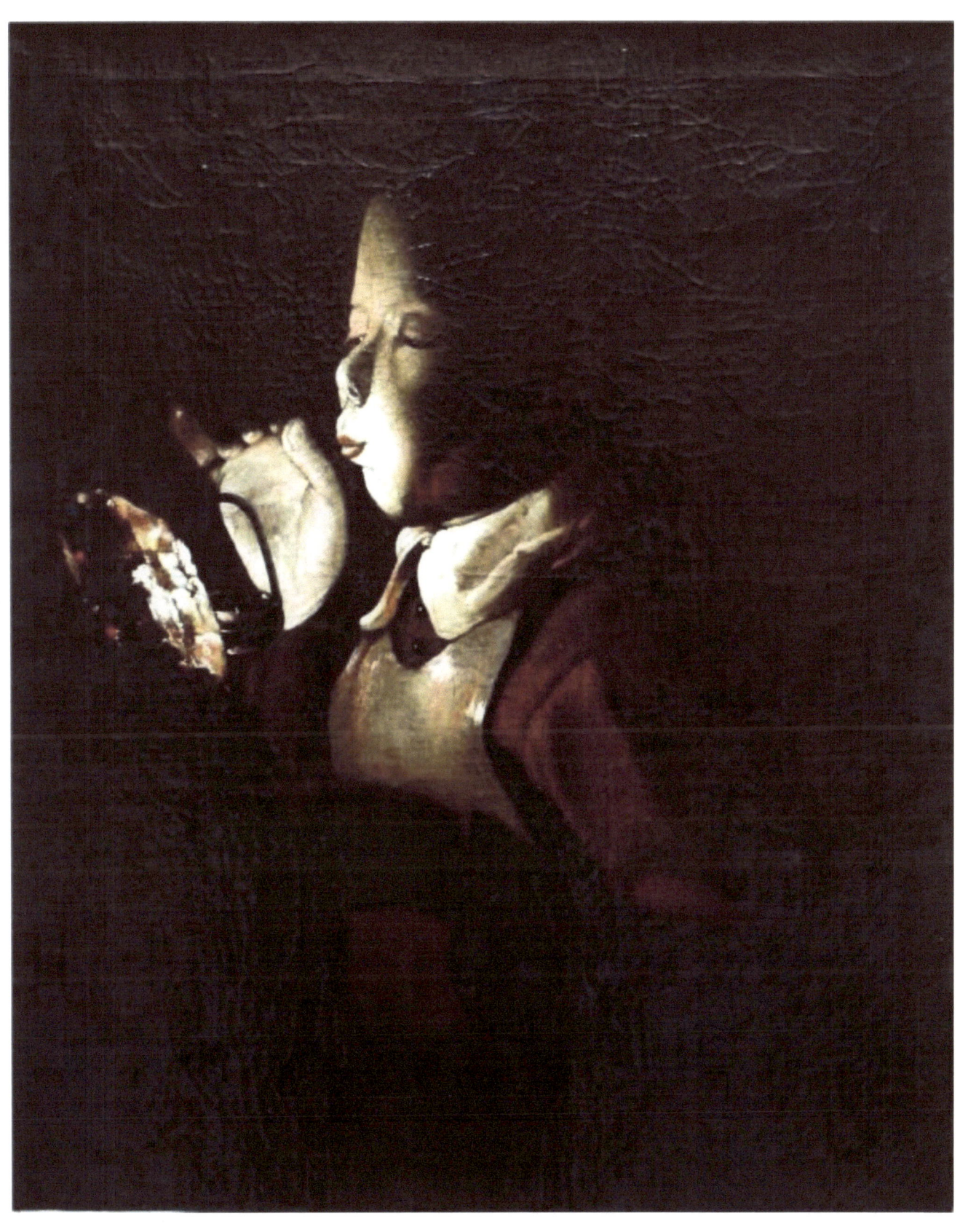

Boy Blowing at Lamp, c.1640, oil on canvas

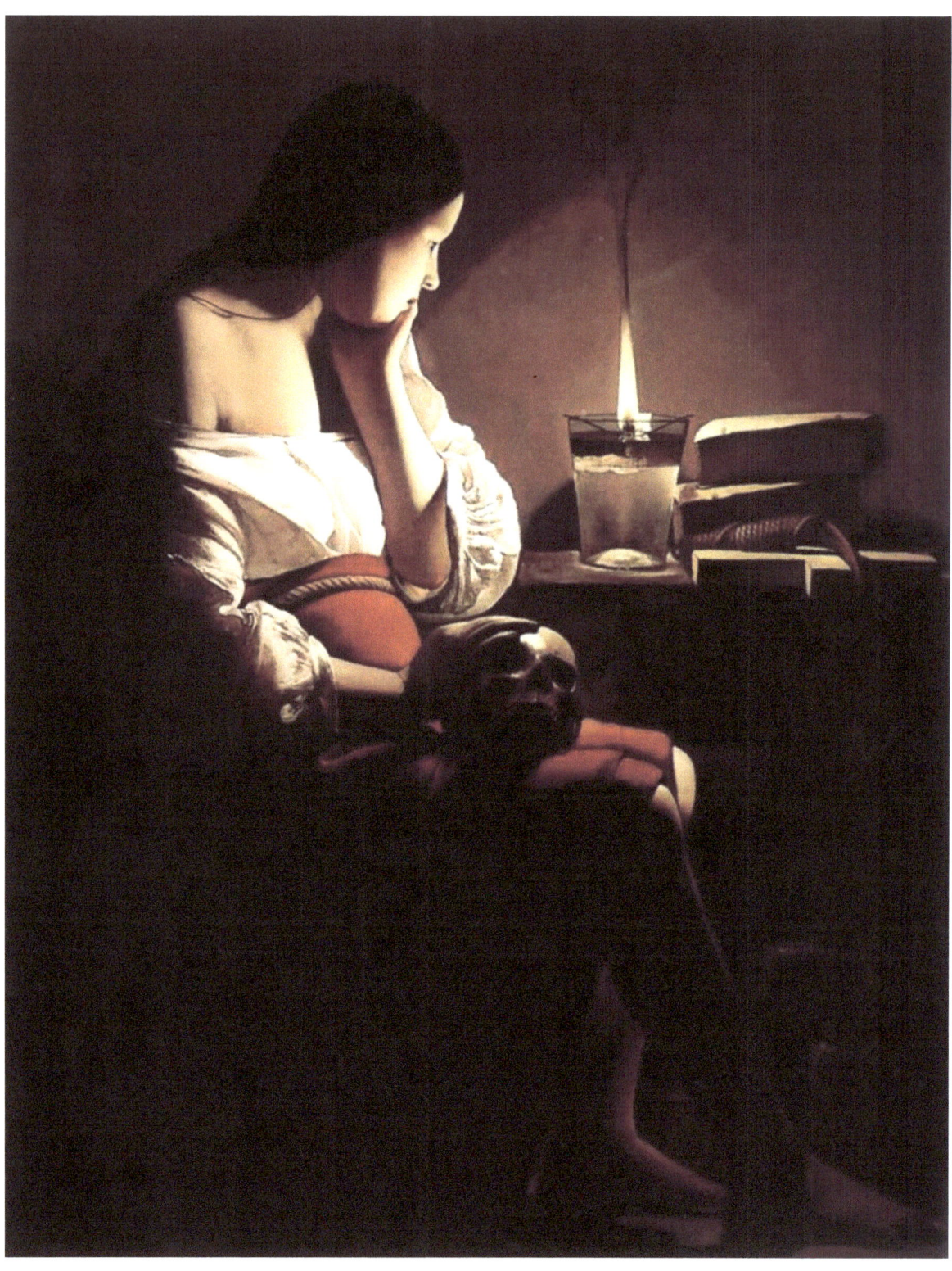

Magdalen with the Smoking Flame, c. 1640, Oil on canvas, 117 x 92 cm

Around 1620 a group of young French painters developed interesting derivations from works by Caravaggio. Among these we find Georges de la Tour. In his canvases he adopted the strong light and shade contrasts characteristics of Caravaggio's school, although in his chiaroscuro effects he preferred the Nordic tenebrosi's use of artificial light, such as candles and torches, which produces a dazzling effect and creates a more transcendental atmosphere that does not include the supernatural.

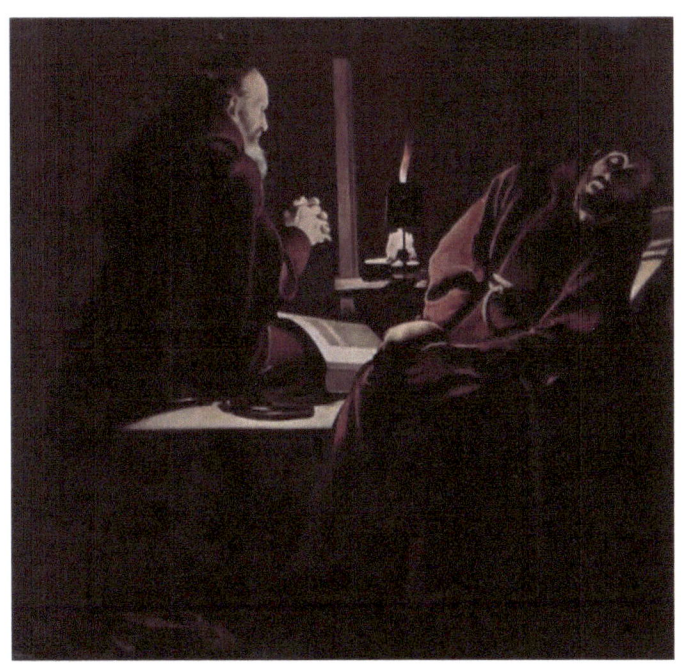

St. Francis in Extasy, also called The Praying Monk beside the Dying Monk, c.1640, oil on canvas

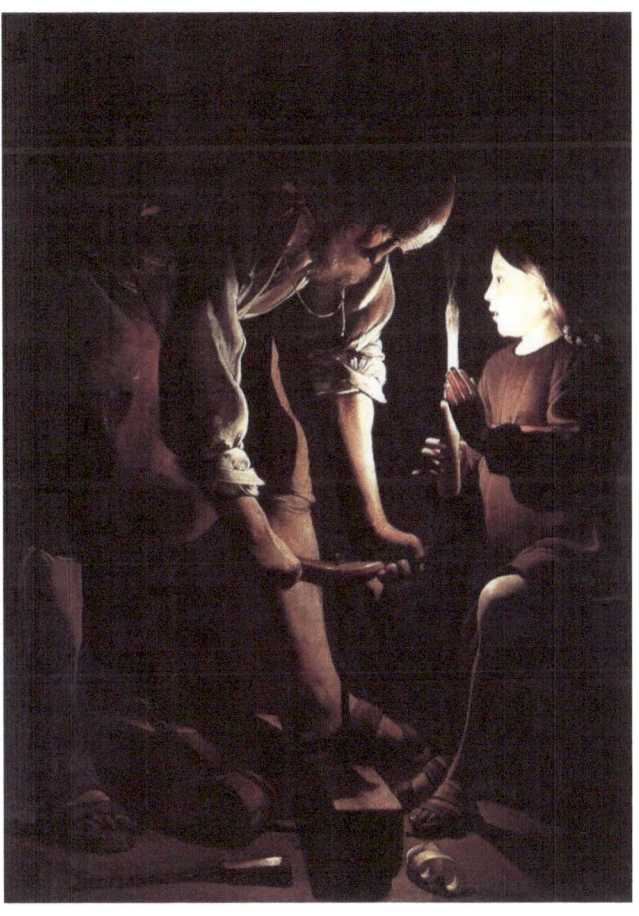

Christ in the Carpenter's Shop, c.1635-1640, oil on canvas

On the same deep level as in the Job, in a similar vein but more complex in composition, is the Christ in the Carpenter's Shop in the Louvre. As in the Job, one of the figures is arched over the top of the canvas, and again the attention to mood is shown in the minute observation of the effects of light in certain areas, especially that of the translucency of the child's hand silhouetted against the candle, revealing even the dirt in the fingernails. As usual, La Tour tells the Bible story in the simplest of terms. Only items essential for identifying the subject, in this case the paraphernalia of the carpenter's shop, are included. The picture can exist on the level of a genre scene without religious overtones, and its realism makes it one of the greatest genre paintings of the seventeenth century, rivaling Velazquez's Water Seller of Seville and Rembrandt's Jewish Bride (the latter has also been interpreted as a religious or mythological subject).

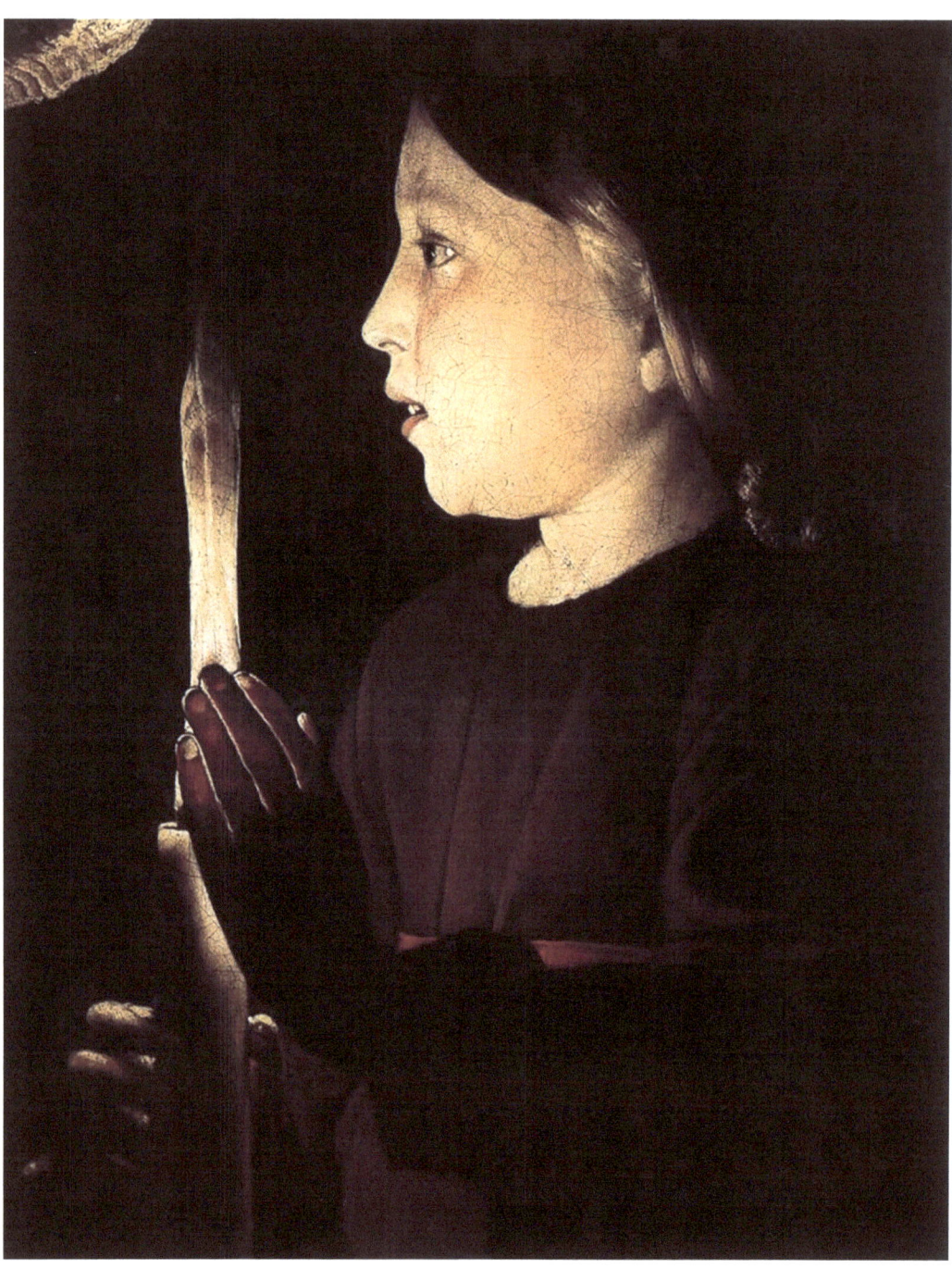

Christ in the Carpenter's Shop (detail)

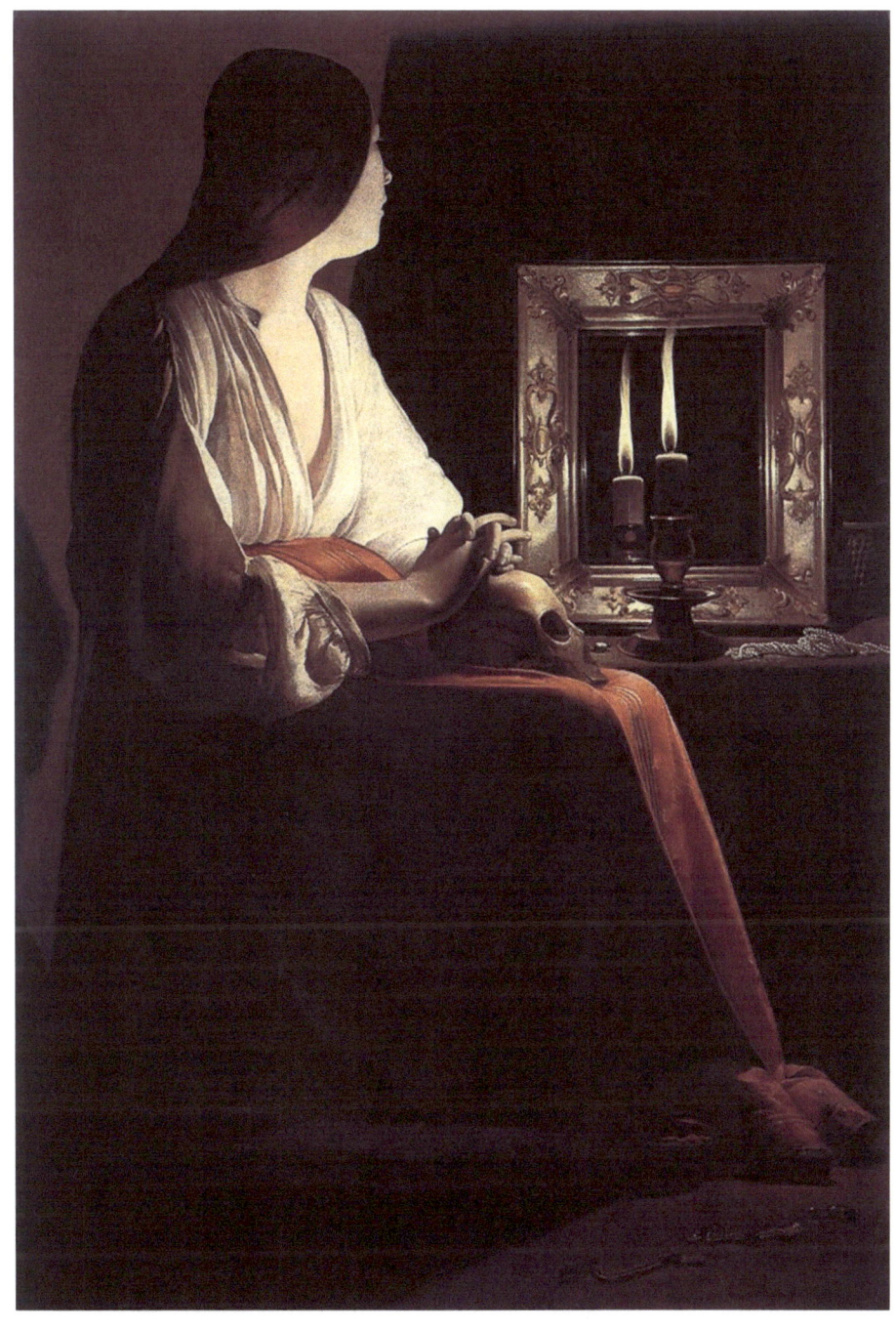

Repenting Magdalene, also called Magdalene and Two Flames, c.1638-1643, oil on canvas

An artist of great brilliance and originality, Georges de La Tour was from the duchy of Lorraine in northeastern France. Early in his career he gained knowledge of contemporary Caravaggesque painting with its emphasis on realism and dramatic effects of light and dark. This picture shows Mary Magdalen in a dark room at the dramatic moment of her conversion, her features lit by a candle flame that imparts a hauntingly spiritual quality to the work. The elaborate silver mirror, the pearls on the table, and the jewels on the floor symbolize luxury, which she has cast aside. In their place she clasps a skull, a common symbol of mortality.

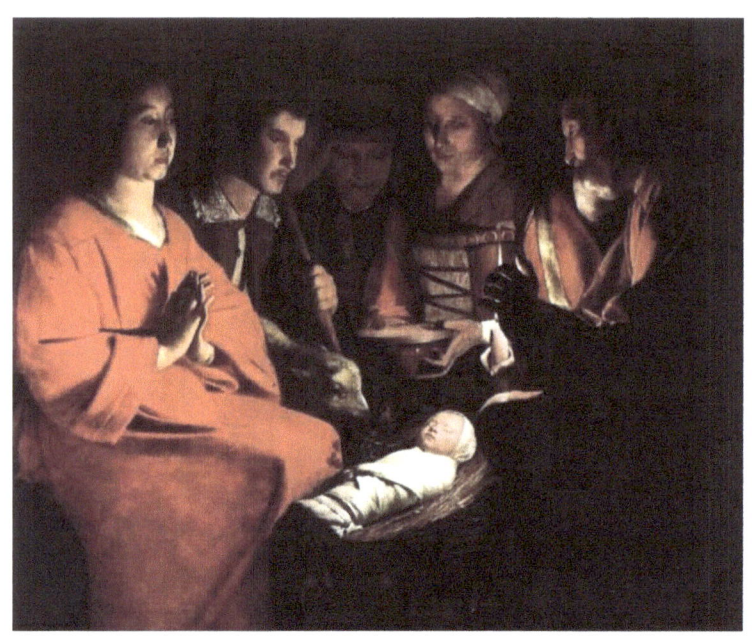

Adoration of the Shepherds, c.1644, oil on canvas

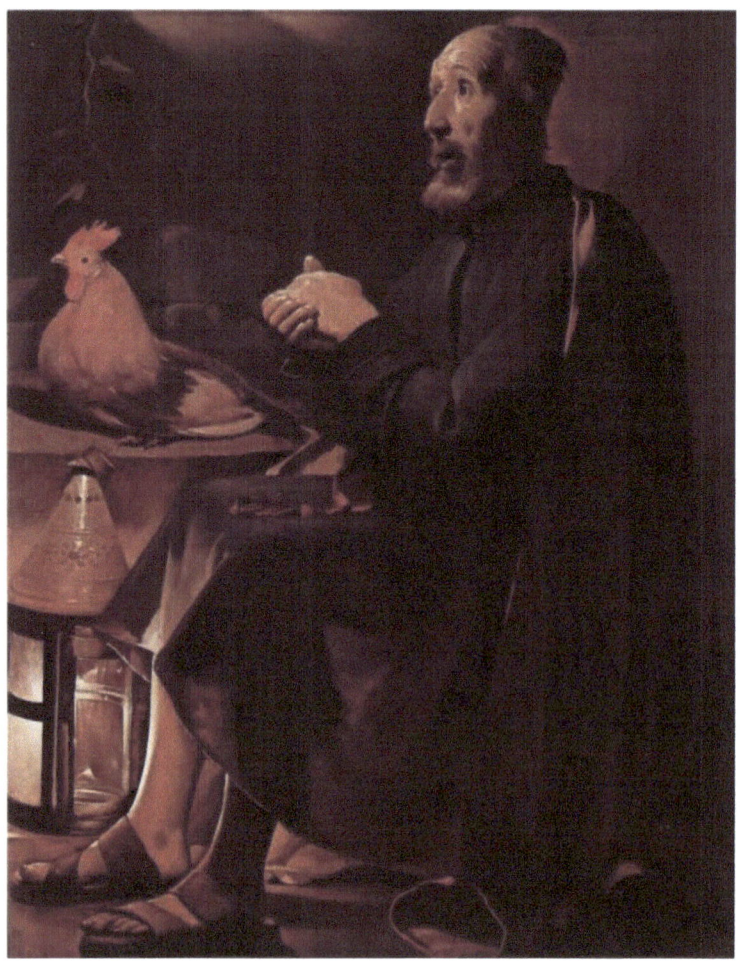

The Tears of St. Peter, also called Repenting of St. Peter, 1645, oil on canvas

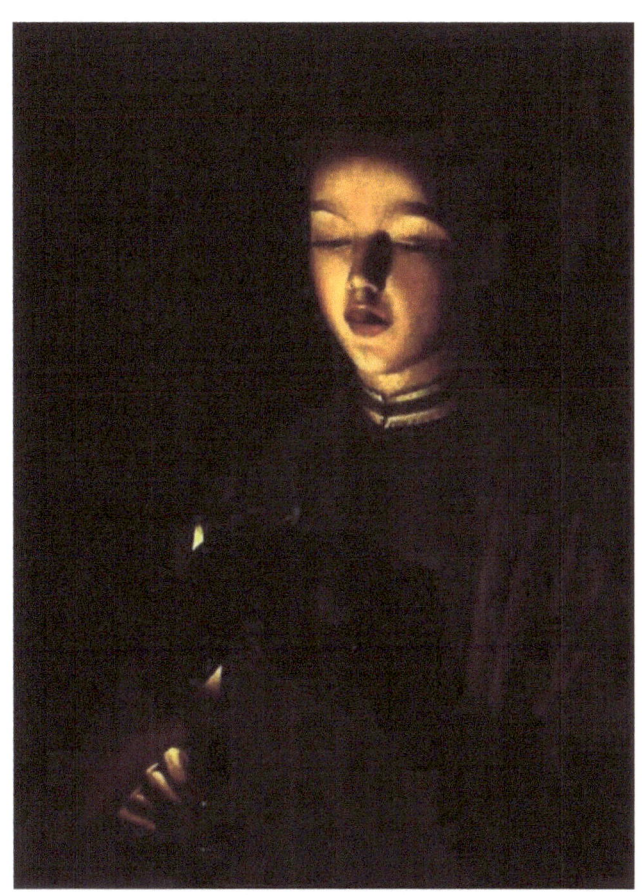

The Young Singer, c.1640-c.1645, oil on canvas

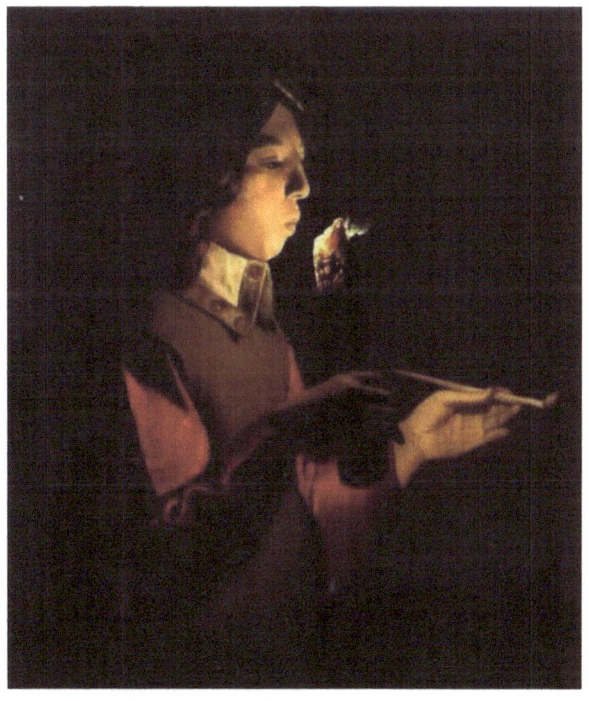

Blower with a Pipe, 1646, oil on canvas

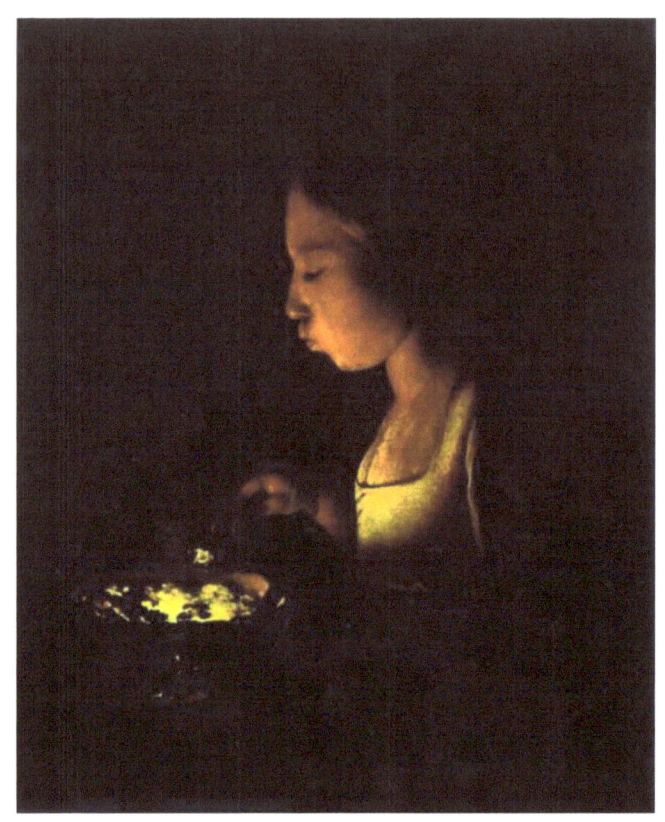

Girl with a Brazier, 1646-1648, oil on canvas

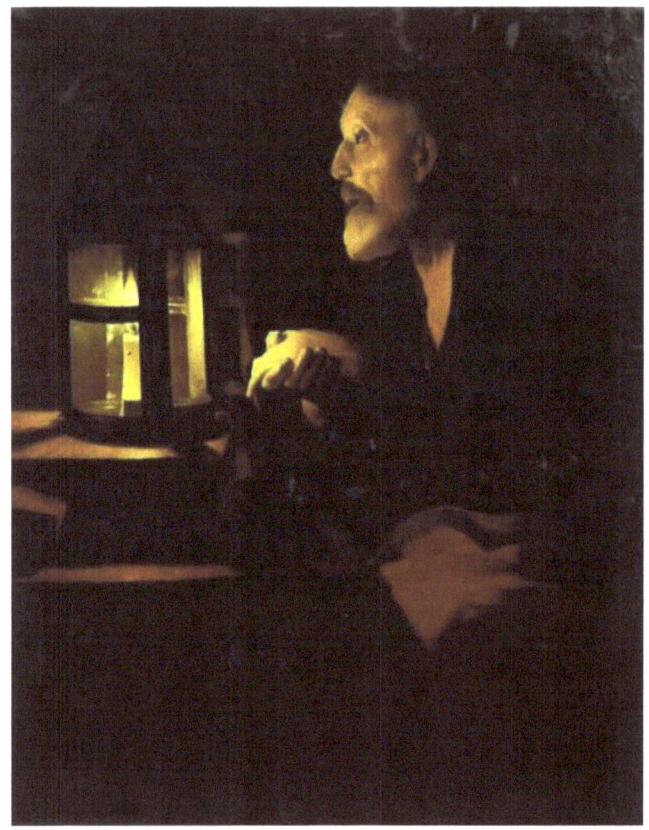

Tears of St. Peter, 1646-1648, oil on canvas

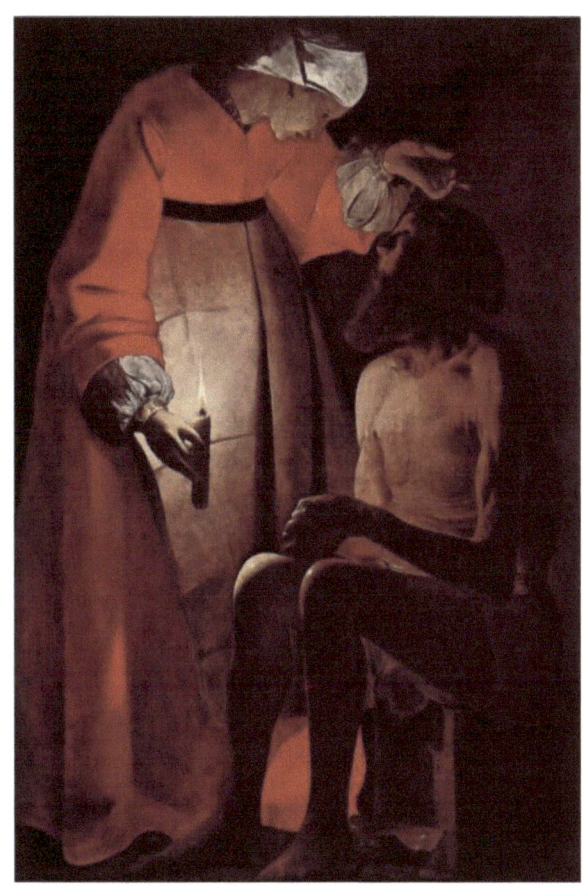

Job Mocked by His Wife, 1625-1650, oil on canvas

There was a change in La Tour's style from the morbidity and mystery of such pictures as the penitent Magdalen contemplating a skull and a monk watching over his dead or dying companion, to works of a much calmer and more distilled air. The transitional pictures, also datable to the 1630s, are Job Mocked by his Wife at Йpinal and the so-called 'Woman with the Flea' at Nancy.

The composition of the Job is immediately striking. There is the same flickering movement that is found in the Payment of Dues, even though there are only two figures. It is derived from Bellange's etching of The Annunciation. an unexpected source, especially when it is considered that The Annunciation by Caravaggio was already in the ducal collection at Nancy by 1616 (this much-damaged picture is now in the Musйe des Beaux-Arts at Nancy where it is accepted by most authorities as authentic). No influence on La Tour is discernible in the Caravaggio, although it is virtually certain that he knew it.

The subject is a rare one, and La Tour has introduced a special pathos into Job's sufferings. Although its composition is a complex amalgam of the Bellange Annunciation, the mood of the Job is entirely original. La Tour has concentrated on a dialogue between the unfortunate Job and his ill-tempered wife, and has allowed us a glimpse of a rarely painted subject, a husband tormented by his wife. Her cruel mockery of him comes over with great force as Job sits helplessly contemplating his sores (the potsherd he uses to scrape them is on the ground). The spectator is forced to realize that this painter's genius lies chiefly in his ability to observe the human condition; his skill in painting candlelight is only part of the brilliance. Such a depiction of the complex relationship between two people is rare indeed in French art of the period, and in his maturity La Tour was to develop the concept of dialogue between people to ever-increasing heights of subtlety.

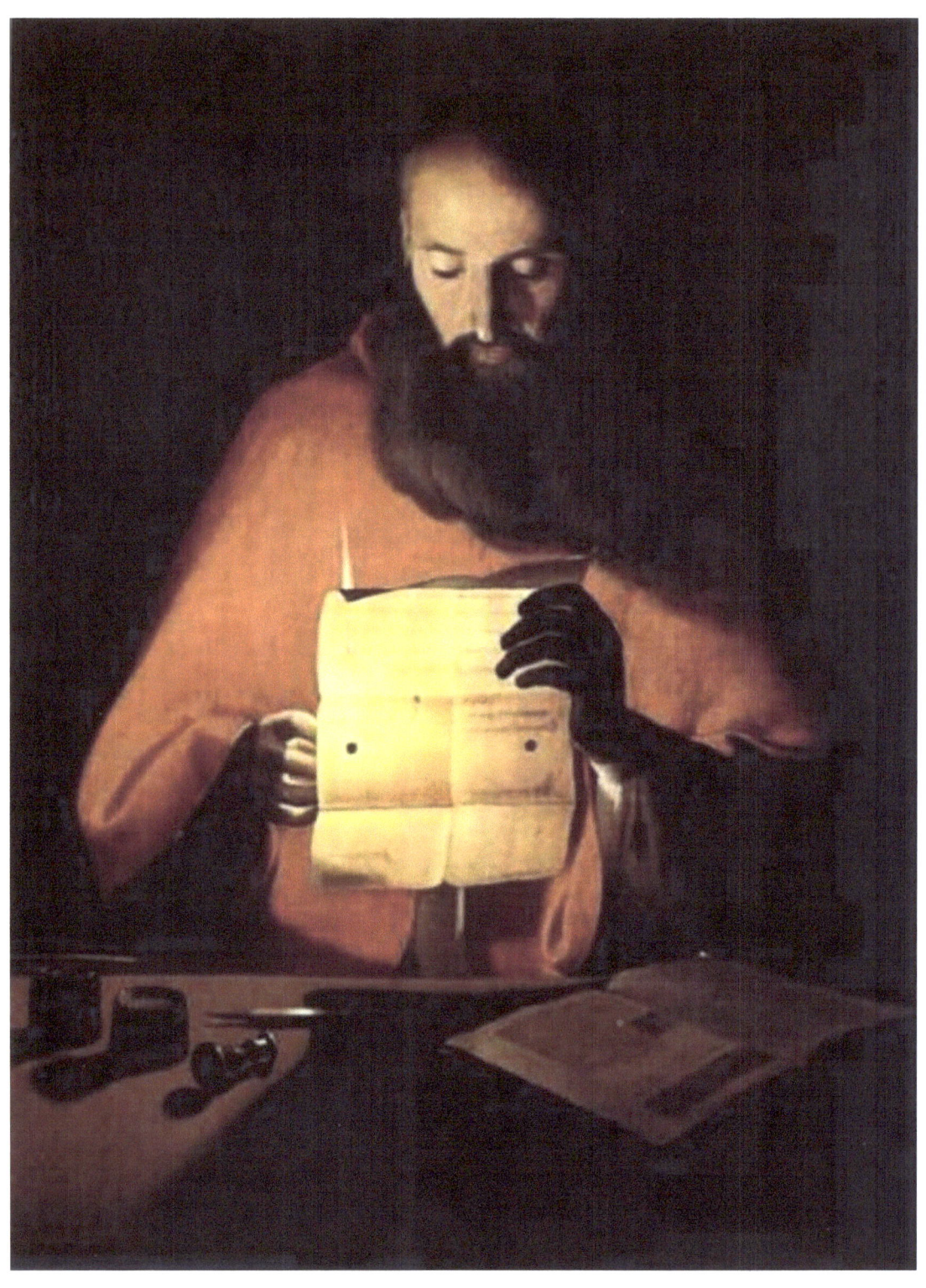

St. Jerome Reading, 1648-1650, oil on canvas

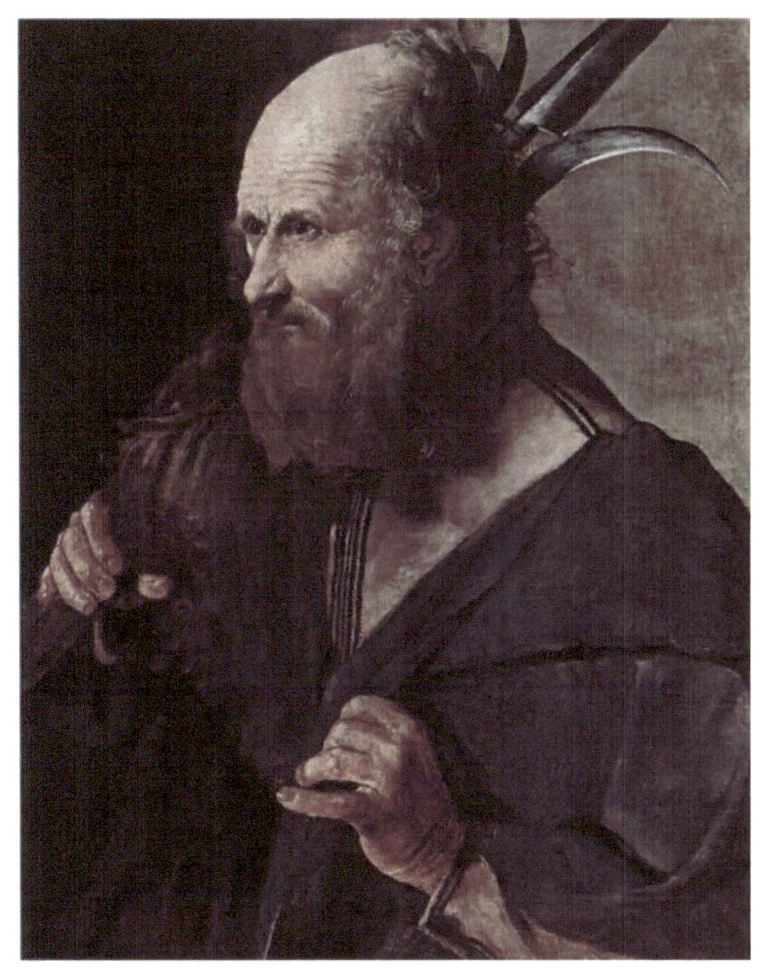

St. Jude Thaddeus, 1624-1650, oil on canvas

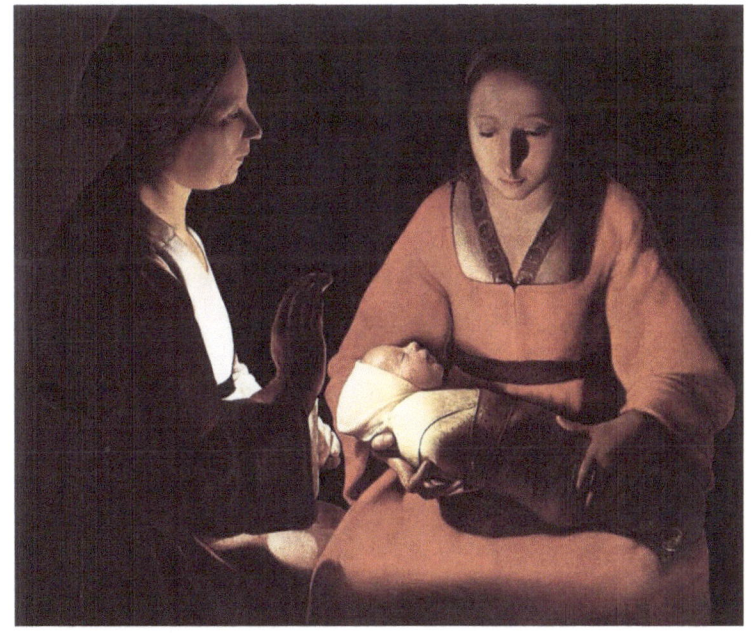

The New-born, 1640s, Oil on canvas, 76 x 91 cm

The subject is ambiguous because the spectator is uncertain whether it is a simple genre scene or whether it represents the Virgin, St Anne and the Christ Child.

By common consent La Tour's best picture is the New-born. At first sight this now-famous work seems starkly simple, a refinement of the already-familiar mannerisms and abbreviations, and only close inspection of the relatively small-scale picture reveals its complexity. The technique is almost pointiliste: the intense red of the mother's dress is achieved by minute dots of colour of varying hue, and the same is true of the lilac garment of the servant (or St Anne, if the subject is the Christ Child). The whole surface is thus the product of an intensely concentrated effort, and a large amount of detail is concealed in the stark simplicity of the forms. The collar of the mother's dress is elaborately decorated, and the profiles are painted with an exceptional delicacy of line.

A total calm pervades the picture, in which the faces have been described as almost Buddha-like in their serenity. The sentiments which characterize almost all the rest of seventeenth-century painting are avoided, and this picture alone justifies La Tour's reputation. Just as Vermeeer's View of Delft is exceptional, even for Vermeer, so the New-born raises above all the conventions of its time.

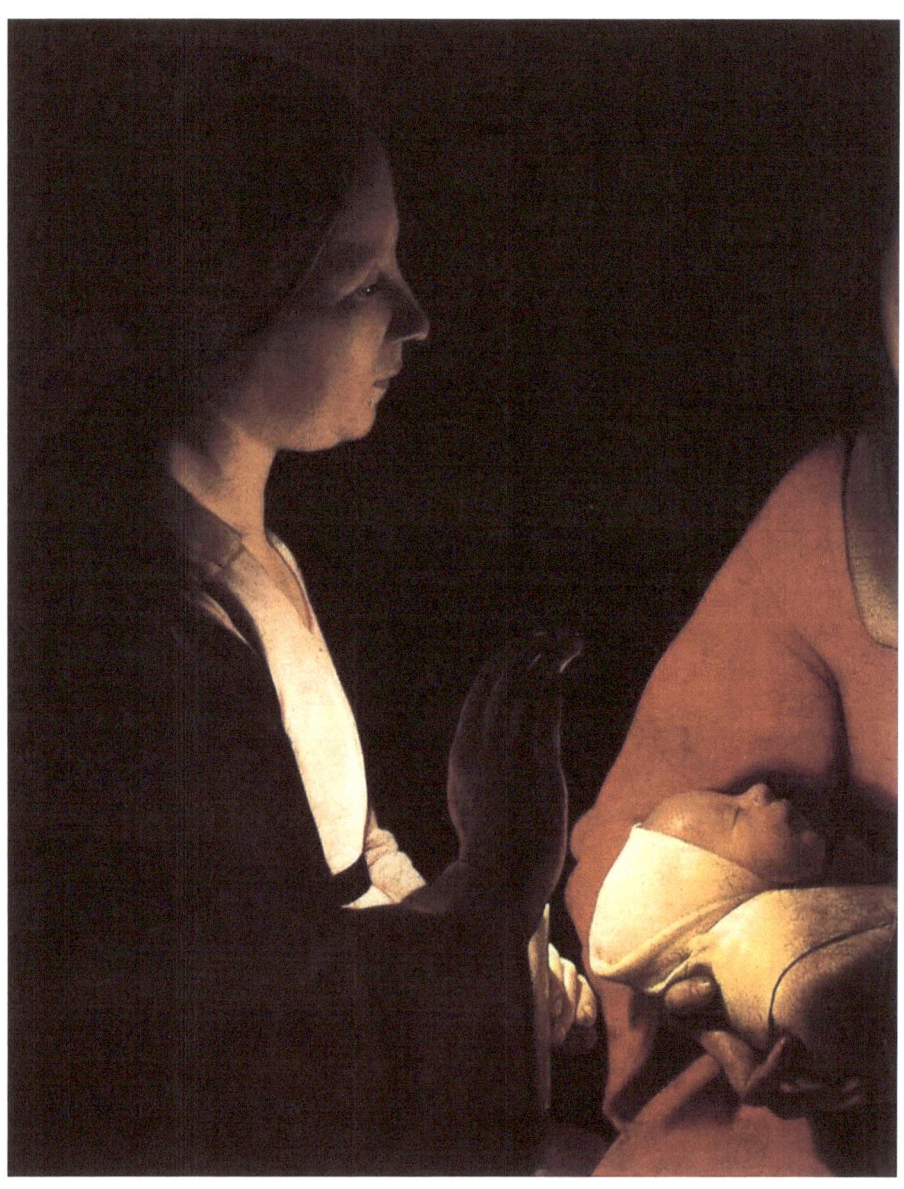

The New-born (detail)

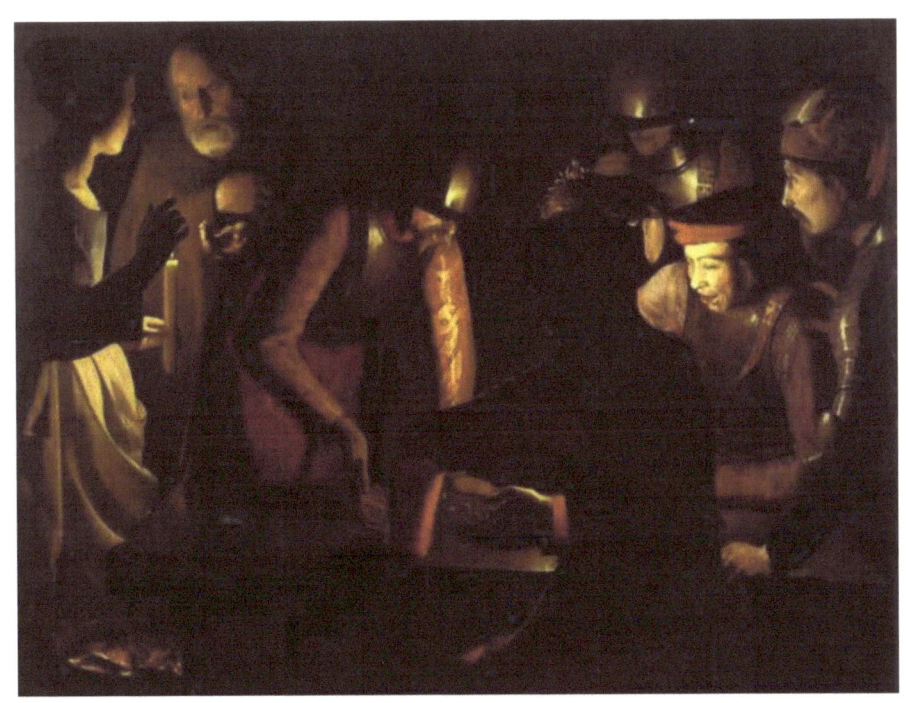

The Denial of St. Peter, 1650, oil on canvas

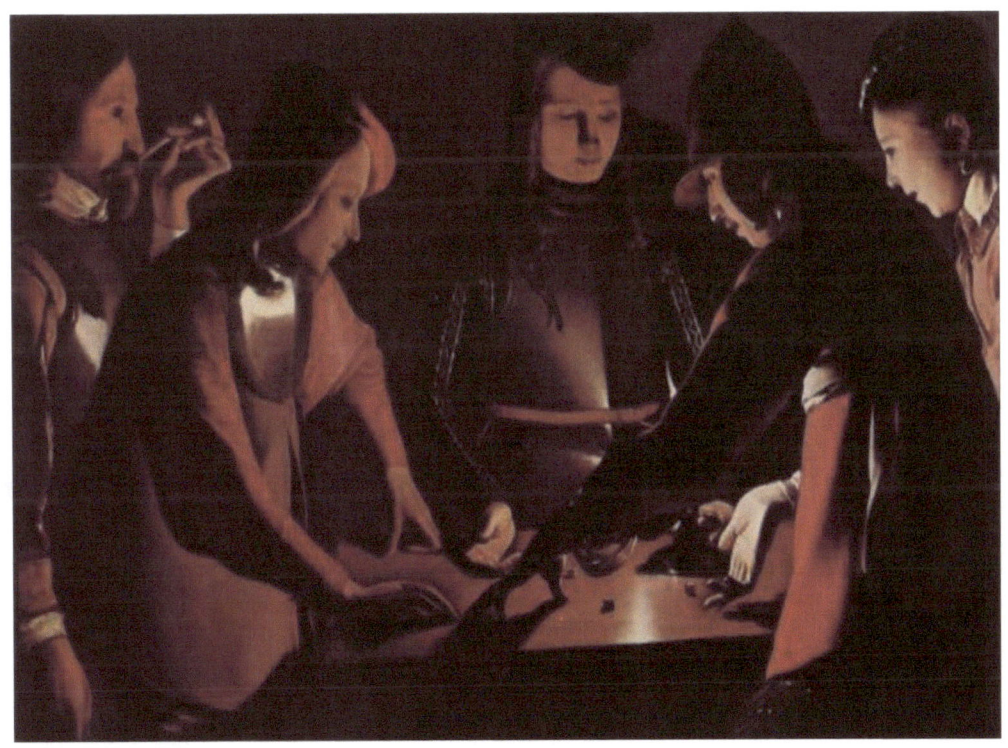

The Dice Players, 1650-1651, oil on canvas

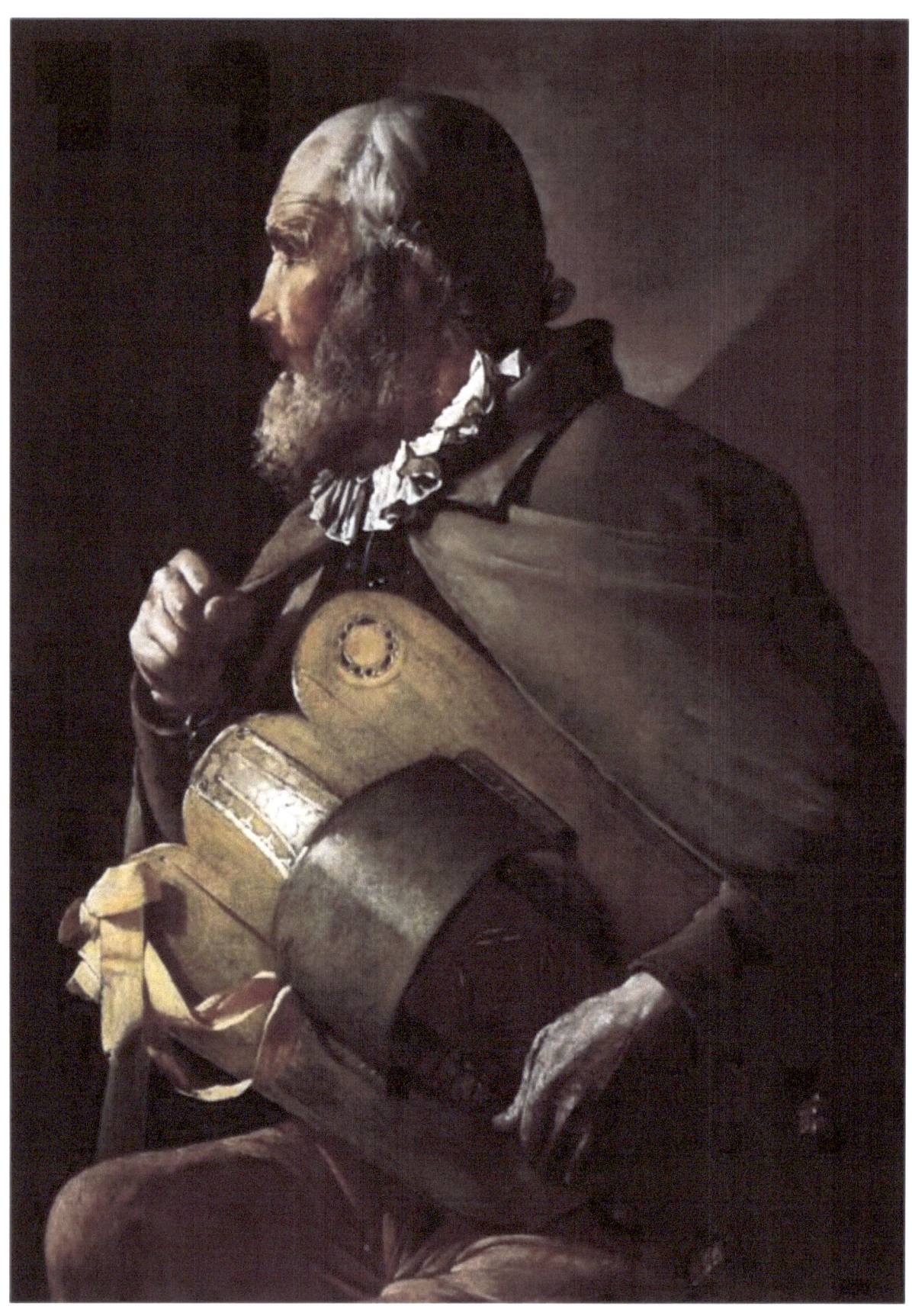

The Blind Hurdy Gurdy Player, oil on canvas

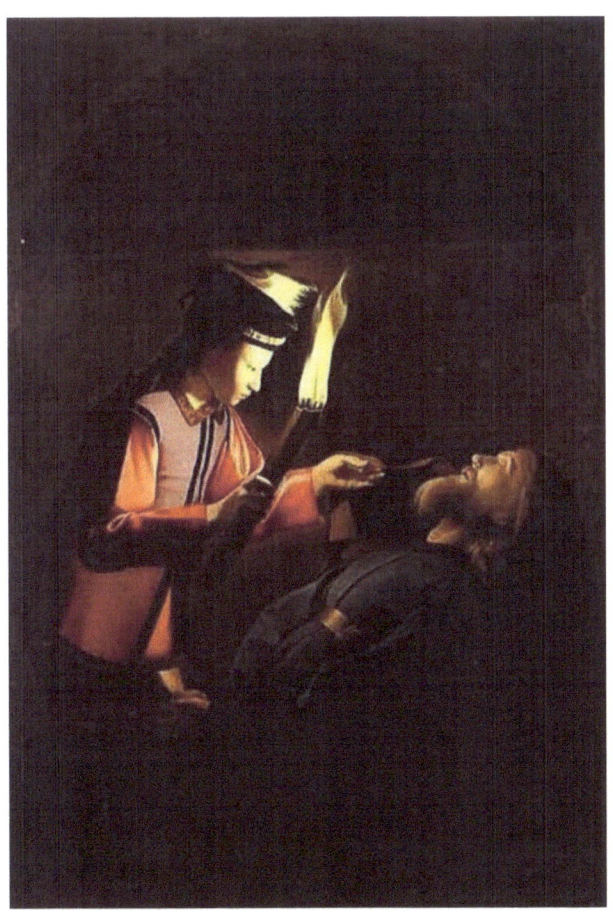

The Discovery of the Body of St. Alexis, oil on canvas

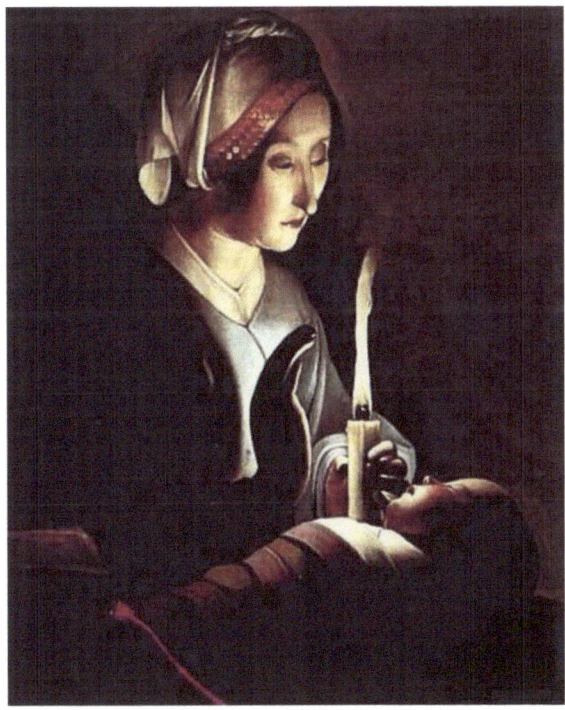

The Newborn, also called St. Anne and the Virgin in Linen, oil on canvas

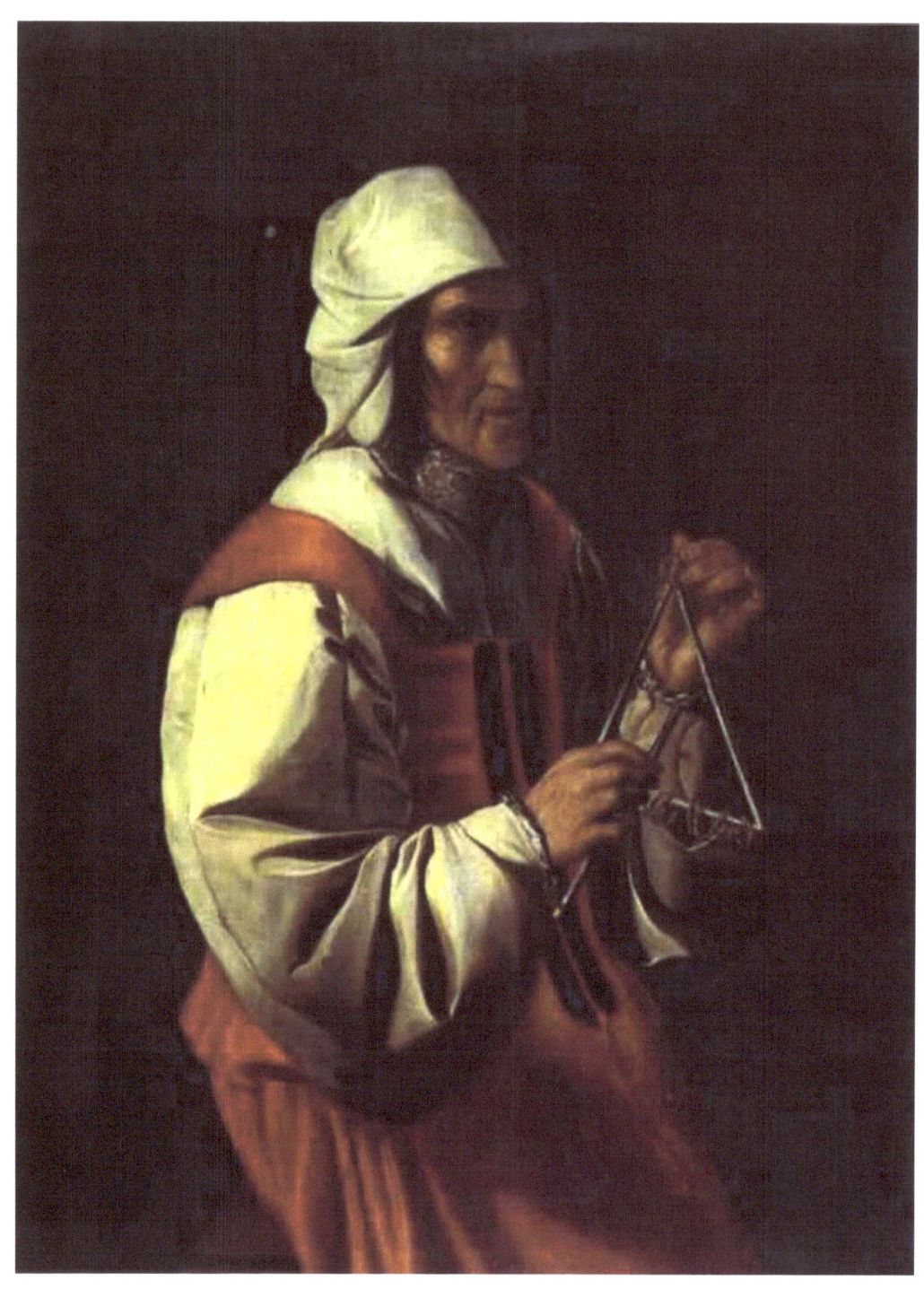

The Triangle Player, oil on canvas

www.ingramcontent.com/pod-product-compliance
Lightning Source LLC
Chambersburg PA
CBHW050355180526
45159CB00005B/2030